LOOKING BACK

Glimpses of
My Past

By Danny Henderson

Dear Graham and Marry Lou,
I won't even try to put into words
what your friend ship hes ment to
me. God sunley smiles when he
sees you two.

So do I
I love you,
your friend
Danny

1

7-24-17

LOOKING BACK
Glimpses of My Past

As Told to Victor Kelly, Sr.

Copyright 2017
Cover design by Phoenix Publishing

Published by Phoenix Publishing Group

www.phoenixpublishinggroup.net

Printed in the United States of America
First Edition 2016
ISBN 978-0-9802279-3-2

Table of Contents

Part 1: Chapters in My Life

Part II
Memories in My Heart

Part III
New Directions

Foreword

Danny became my friend from very near the first days that my family arrived in Phoenix in 1952 and when I enrolled in Phoenix Christian High School. He was the "wild and woolly" one in our class, and I was the "conservative" one in our group which included Walter Arnold and so many others. At Phoenix Christian we studied together and played on the Basketball and Football teams. Danny's mom had become friends with the Argabrights, and Danny drove their daughter, Mary Lou to school every day for two years. Mary Lou later became my wife.

In this book Danny writes about his adventures, both big and small. The incredible stories of travel to faraway places which he pursued with an energy and enthusiasm for "Experiencing the world" amazed me as well as many of his friends. What struck us more was that Danny actually had the drive to live things that others only dream about.

While learning about his the experiences is fascinating, the reader sees Danny's boundless enthusiasm for learning and making new friends is what shines through.   Danny loves people with a force so natural, it exudes from his pores.

His love of risk-taking took him to so many dangerous adventures that even he himself was surprised at his actions – some of which were fun, and others which were often ridiculously dangerous.   Over the years, as I came together with Danny from time to time, I could sense that beneath it all, there was never a time when Danny was not aware of the foundation of God in his Life. During our visits Danny often spoke with me about needing to change his life's direction. Along with the excitement he experienced, he was concerned about and regretted the sadness he felt he may have created by his impulsive behaviors. Through everything, Danny's love for his family was deep and real, and he was proud of their work ethic and of how smart they were.

As his friend, along with others, I wondered how to help Danny "Grow Up!" In Danny's Friday night Canasta group of old school friends and our mates, we could see that beneath all the energy, adventure, and spontaneity, Danny was really wanting to rearrange his life to be more predictable and understandable, and that was always a vital part of our conversations. In spite of his crazy ways and adventures, we all loved him.

How to explain a man who did so much with such creativity and excellence that others would be attracted to and yield themselves up to him is difficult. In search of a special tile for his business in Las Vegas, Danny traveled halfway around the world to Japan and made friends with a complete stranger who provided contacts with tile suppliers. That business arrangement lasted for almost forty years. As Danny's pool business grew, he worked for and made friends with celebrities in Las Vegas, among whom were Seigfried and Roy, Ed Winn, Liberace, Phyllis Diller, Roy Rogers, Mike Tyson, and many others.

Even with the satisfaction of the successes, and his travels, Danny still felt an emptiness that has started with a failed marriage and developed into a loneliness that simply would not go away. Then he met Joannie Appellof.

When Joannie came into Danny's life, she impacted every part of who he was. Having found Christ some twenty-five years before, Joannie had the depth and wisdom to see beyond Danny's "craziness" to a deeper, hungry man who longed to return to his spiritual roots. Joanie encouraged him to share with her a deep continuous discovery of spiritual truths she was learning in the Scriptures. Danny embraced Joannie and reconnected with his friends to once again share their lives as well.

There was one other change. Danny had always watched out for his brother, Bill, always seeking to be with him through some of Bill's most difficult times in his emotional life; and he often resented that role. But now his attitude changed from simply family duty and obligation to a deep love and a Christ-like consistency.

Part Three ends this book; but it begins a new story in the process of being told.

Graham Reedy, M.D.

PART I

Chapters in My Life

Because it rains when we wish it wouldn't

Because men do what they often shouldn't

Because crops fail, and plans go wrong –

Some of us grumble all day long.

But somehow, in spite of the care and doubt,

It seems at last all things work out.

--Edgar A. Guest

Beginnings

Family

My Great-Grandfather on my mother's side, William Fletcher Snider, was born on December 26, 1840, and he died in 1924 in Rankin County, Mississippi. William married Martha Jane Howard, born January 11, 1843 in Bibb County, Alabama. Martha Jane died in 1898.

William and Martha had two children, William and Jesse A. Snider. Jesse was born in Panola County, Texas, March 21, 1870. He was my Grandfather and died on August 19, 1957.

Jesse married my Grandmother, Mildred Lindsey Lancaster, born in Chickasaw County, Mississippi, on August 31, 1880. She died in Phoenix, Arizona in December, 1965. Her father was Abe N. Lancaster, born November 4, 1834, and he died in 1890 in Spartenburg, South Carolina. My Great-Grandmother, Jane E Golightly, was born on December 12, 1841 and died in 1915.

My Grandpa on my mother's side, Jesse Ada Snider, born in Chickasaw, Texas, and Granny, Mildred Lindsey Lancaster, born in Mississippi, were children of sharecroppers in the mid 1800's.

My grandfather on my father's side, Robert E. Lee Henderson, was born in Piedmont, Calhoun County, Alabama in 1864. He was married to Samantha Ann Turner, also born in Piedmont. They had five children: Jim, Tandy, Mary-Ann, my dad, Robert Gaither, and my dad's brother – my uncle, Gaston. My Dad, Robert Gather Henderson, was born on July 31, 1889. After my

Dad's mother died in Calhoun in 1896, the family moved and went westward.

HENDERSON FAMILY TREE

GENERATION 1 **GENERATION 2** **GENERATION 3** **GENERATION 4**

Martha Jane Howard
b. 1843 - d. 1898

married

William Flecher Snider
b. 1840 - d. 1924

Jesse Ada Snider
b. Mar 21, 1870, Texas
d. Aug 19, 1957, Phx, AZ

married

Abe Lancaster
b. 1838 - d. 1890

married

Jane Elizabeth Golightly
b. 1841 - d. 1915

Mildred Lindsey Lancaster "Granny"
b. Aug 31, 1880, Mississippi
d. Dec. 1965, Phx, AZ

Robert E Lee Henderson
b. 1864, Piedmont, AL.
d. 193?, Phx, AZ

married

Samantha Ann Turner
b. ?   d. 1896

Effie
b. ___, 1884   d. 1960

Lois Snider
b. Sept 29, 1899 Mineral Wells, TX
d. Jan 5, 1956, Phoenix, AZ

married

Robert Gather Henderson
b. Jul 31, 1889, Calhoun, AL
d. Oct 10, 1959, Phoenix, AZ

Jim
b. 1893   d. 1960

Tandy
b. 1894   d 1950

Mary-Ann
b. 1884   d. ?

Gaston
b. 1893   d. 1955?

Helen Inez
b. June 13, 1918
d. ___, 2001

Imogene
b. Dec 10, 1919
d. ___, 2012

Fredna Jane
b. Sep 3, 1922
d. ___, 1968

Jimmy Dale
b. 1930
d. 1932

Robert "Daniel"
b. Dec 31, 1936
d.

William Richard
b. Feb 4, 1939
d.

Henderson Family Tree

I know only fragments of my grandfather's life, but from the stories I heard while growing up, it was colorful. My grandfather on my father's side was married four times. He spent a year in the penitentiary for making "Moonshine" in hidden illegal stills. About 1899, when my dad was ten years old, the family finally ended up in Mineral Wells, Texas.

At that time Mineral Wells, located about fifty miles west of Fort Worth, was a small town of about 2,000 in population. It was named for the nearby mineral springs which were supposed to have healthful effects, and over the following two decades people from all over the world came to the springs to seek relief from various maladies.

Gibson Well, Mineral Wells, Texas.

Mineral Wells about the turn of the 20th Century

(University of North Texas Libraries

Boyce Ditto Public Library)

Growing up in Mineral Wells as a child, my Dad played on unpaved streets and saw the evolution from horse-and-buggy to the chugging of early automobiles. Summers were hot and humid, and winters were mild.

There was no radio or television in those days. People provided their own entertainment, and a natural outlet was music. Mineral Wells had a dance hall, and as a young man, my dad played the fiddle in a honkytonk band on Saturday nights. That's where he met my mother, Lois Snyder. They fell in love and married sometime in 1915- 1916. My Dad was twenty-six, and his bride was sixteen. My Dad's brother, Gaston, married my mother's sister, Effie, and we became double cousins.

Because my dad had asthma, the doctor told him he had to get to a dryer climate. It was 1917, the year America entered the First World War, and my Dad was twenty-eight. Leaving their wives behind, Dad and his brother, Gaston, hopped a freight train and headed for San Bernardino, California, in hopes of working the crops there. Getting kicked off the train in Tucson, they walked over ninety miles to Maricopa, Arizona. Hopping another train, they finally reached California. Deciding to stay in California, they returned to Mineral Wells and packed up their families and possessions.

Moving West

Heading west in 1917, the caravan of several vehicles must have seemed like a latter-day "wagon train" as the two families with their several vehicles chugged under heavy loads along the mostly gravel roads toward California. I remember my father telling about the "corduroy" plank roads as they entered the sand dunes area near Yuma, Arizona. The plank road, stretching from Yuma to Palm Springs, was a one-way route, and at every half-mile, there was a turnout so cars headed in the opposite direction could get by. When they had a flat tire, the inner-tube was often impossible to repair. Tearing out the inner-tube, they stuffed cotton seed in the tire to make is usable again, and continued on their way.

Corduroy road near Yuma

(image from San Diego Blog archive)

The California move was short-lived. The dust and pollen from harvesting crops in the San Bernardino Valley caused my father great distress. Often subject to repeated asthma attacks, he often coughed and wheezed his way through a day's harvest. As he endured those attacks day after day under the California sun, he remembered that he once told his brother that he had, "...Never felt better in his life . . .." than the way he had felt in Phoenix when he and Gaston had made their first trip to California. He spoke to his brother, and they decided to move their families to Phoenix.

Both brothers returned to Mineral Wells, packed up what they couldn't sell or give away of their possessions, and they formed another 1918 "wagon train" for their trek of over nine hundred miles to Phoenix. Chugging over mostly dirt and gravel roads they drove for several days, stopping by the side of the road each night to set up a makeshift camp.

Arriving in Phoenix, with the funds they acquired from the sale of much of their equipment in Texas, they bought a tent and staked it out on Second Avenue in Phoenix. They soon found work as share-croppers on a forty-acre quarter section near 44th Street and Thomas.

In a field like this, my father could pick over 450 pounds of cotton a day.
(image public domain)

My Dad was extremely thrifty. He could earn $10.00 and save $9.95. During and after World War I, there was a cotton boom in the Phoenix area and a labor shortage in the cotton fields. Wages were low for field-workers, but a loaf of bread cost only ten-cents, a gallon of milk only sixty-two cents, and a dozen eggs only thirty-eight cents. Both brothers and Grandpa Snider worked hard, and both families were fed. Even with his asthma, my Dad could pick 450 pounds of cotton a day. In those days, field-workers were paid less than a dollar for every hundred pounds of cotton they picked. Even on those meager wages, my Dad saved every penny he could.

Although the Phoenix climate gave my Dad some relief, working in the fields still caused breathing difficulty, and from the very first time that he had returned to the Salt River Valley, even while still living in the tent, immediately he started planning another way to make a living.

Bob's Transfer and Storage

My dad still had the pickup truck that had carried them back from California, and he used that as a start. He applied for and obtained his Common Carrier license. Next, he converted the pick-up into a flatbed, painted "Bob's Transfer and Storage" on the doors and, in 1918, after only a couple of months working in the fields, he went into business for himself.

With money he was able to scrape together from the sale of his possessions in Mineral Wells, plus the little he earned from field-work, my father was able to buy a one-acre plot of land on 207 West Apache Street in Phoenix, less than a half-mile north of the Salt River. The family lived in a tent on that plot until my father had built his first house.

Even after spending all day working at his trucking business, when my Dad came home, he immediately started working to improve his own land. He hired a drilling company to put down a well. Because the water table was much closer to the surface than it is now, they struck water about 300 feet down after only two days of drilling. My Dad was something of a "Picker," and over the years and months he had gathered all kinds of materials and the odds and ends necessary to build his first little one-room cabin on his own land. His family lived in that little house until he built the big house at 207 West Apache.

My family about 1923 My mother, Lois, Helen, Imogene,
My father, and Fredna in front.

My oldest sister was now grown up enough to watch the younger siblings, so my mother went to work at Good Samaritan Hospital.

Phoenix had grown in population from around 15,000 in 1917 to over 29,000 in 1923. With that growth, the Southern Pacific Railroad decided to run a main line through Phoenix, and at Fourth Avenue and Harrison, a new mission-style station was under construction.

My father knew when trains would arrive, and he would wait with his truck to carry passengers, luggage, goods, and other freight to various hotels, meetings, and to other destinations and locations in town.

When he wasn't hauling passengers, luggage, and freight-goods at all hours of the day and night, my father spent every spare hour working on his house and improving his land. In addition to his own home, in the 1920's, he started building rental houses on the one-acre tract. The first two homes, he built himself, using largely materials he had salvaged from his goings and coming around Phoenix. He had a third rental building hauled in complete by a big truck. From 1923 until after World War II, he managed to squeeze a total of eleven buildings onto that one acre. In 1925 he built the big house where I was born.

The family had now grown larger with the births of three of my older sisters, Helen, Imogene, and Fredna. After Fredna, they had Jimmy. Jimmy died when he was eighteen months old. After Jimmy they had my sister, Bobbie-Lou. I came along in 1936, and in 1939, Billy was born. Billy was born with schizophrenia, but we didn't know about that until a little later; but I'm getting ahead of my story.

My father's business was growing, and the family was doing well, but the good times ended abruptly with three blows that staggered my family. The 1929 depression wiped out my parents' savings. By then we had only two other houses on Garfield in addition to the 921 house. One of the two buildings, an uninsured rental house on Garfield, burnt down. That was a severe financial blow. My father never rebuilt on that lot. Then, eighteen-month-old Jimmy died. Beaten down by these losses, my Dad began to drink. Before long, he was a full-blown alcoholic. Fortunately, all through the depression, my father's trucking business not only kept the family solvent, but it grew.

With the birth of Bobbie-Lou in March, 1935, the size of our family increased up to eight.   When I arrived, born on December 31, 1936, in the old house on West Apache Street, our family swelled to nine. All during these years, my father's trucking business had flourished. He had expanded to four trucks and had employed two additional men. My mother still worked in the kitchen at Good Samaritan Hospital.

Here I am, little Danny at three years old

We lived in the old house at 207 West Apache until we moved to the Garfield house in 1940 when I was almost six years old. I loved that old house on Apache and the land around it. The Apache house had an irrigation ditch in front, and beyond the ditch, a cotton field. A wheat field stretched out in back of the house. I spent a lot of time splashing around in the water in the irrigation ditch – especially on hot summer days. My friends and I built a canoe that wouldn't float. Then we tried to float around in a tub, but it had holes in the bottom. We were too little to get into much difficulty, and we had a lot of fun. The cotton fields, also, were not neglected. They provided the battlegrounds for many "cowboy and Indian" skirmishes between me and my friends.

One adventure involving that Apache house stands out in my mind. At first our home on Apache had an outhouse rather than an inside toilet. As a five-year-old I somehow thought it would be fun to drop a little cat through the round hole into the muck below to see what would happen. What a mistake! The cat began to scream and yowl as she dog-paddled in the excrement. My mom heard the screams and ordered me to get the cat out of the crap. I looked around and found a two-by-four about five-feet long and slipped it down into the poop. The cat climbed up onto it, and out she came. She stopped, glared at me and shook the crap off herself to splatter it all over the outhouse and me. I never experimented with the cat again.

After we moved to the house on Garfield, My dad would often take me with him on his trips to the train-station and around town in that old flatbed truck. When we had a load at the train station, on the way, I would see shoeshine boys all over town. That's when I got the idea of becoming a shoeshine boy.

I was only five years old, and I panicked as I thought through my decision to go into business for myself. Starting out with my new shoeshine box, I had all the colors--black, brown, and cordovan. I had a brush, a bottle of soap, and a shine cloth. As I thought about the process of cleaning and polishing the shoes, I stopped and wondered if I was supposed to clean the bottom of the shoes as well. I couldn't remember so I turned around and went home to get more information. I'm sure my Grandpa or my dad had made me my shoeshine box.

My grandpa, Robert E. Lee Henderson

My family was doing fine. We now had six rental houses, and dad's trucking business was doing well. In addition, my dad was careful with his finances and wise in investing. Every time he gathered two or three-thousand dollars, he would invest it in a rental property. By the time he died, he had acquired six rental houses.

Grade School

We had moved into the Garfield house in 1940. Then Pearl Harbor was attacked December 7, 1941. The September before, I had started at Garfield grade school, just three blocks from my home. Garfield Grade School went only to the fifth grade, and I loved going there through all five grades. I was William Tell in the school play. I was marble champ, and I was lieutenant in the Junior Police. Then, in 1946 I started sixth grade at Edison school on Eighteenth Street and Roosevelt.

Edison was a brand-new school, and I loved it. I was popular at Edison, and when I was in the eighth grade, I was elected Student-Council President. The things I learned in Student Council about how to work with others proved invaluable and helped set the direction for what I would do in later life.

At Edison, I especially loved the woodworking shop where one of my favorite teachers, Mr. Clements, taught me to use tools and to work with wood. He was one of the most dedicated teachers I have ever met. My last project was that of making wooden gun cabinet. When graduation time came at Edison school, I had still not finished it. Mr. Clements came in after the school year ended and helped me complete my project. I will always remember him for that. I still have that gun cabinet, and it is filled with my favorite shotguns.

My gun cabinet brings back great memories
of Edison School

The next life-changing force for me was my
family's involvement in the First Missionary Church in
Phoenix.

Church

First Missionary Church (photo © GNU Free Documentation License)

One of the families befriending us when we moved to Garfield Street was the Augabrites. As the relationship developed, they invited our family to visit the First Missionary Church on 902 E. McKinley Street. Over the course of time, in 1947, my mother, and my brother Bill, all felt our need for salvation, and we went forward to accept Christ as our personal Savior.

That event transformed the tone and direction of our whole family. Our attitudes changed radically, especially my Mom's.

My mother became a transformed woman. I never heard her curse again. She eagerly went to church every time the doors were open and immersed herself in church activities and ministries. She enthusiastically attended Bible-studies and prayer meetings and looked forward to the pot-lucks. She eagerly shared the Gospel with others and joyfully told them what God had done for her. Often at prayer meeting, she would stand up and say, "Please, pray for my boys. Please pray for my two boys." God was in control of her life.

Our lives revolved around the church. Even my Dad started to attend, but by now his asthma had advanced to the point that he wheezed so loudly that he could be heard throughout the whole church. Having frequent coughing fits, he would sit at the back of the church so he could slip out when he felt the spasms coming on. He wasn't as outspoken about his faith as Mom was, and that motivated Reverend Garig to ask him outright if he had accepted Christ as Savior. My father assured him that he had.

There weren't as many of us at home, now. My three oldest sisters had married and had moved away, and our family now consisted of my parents, Billie, Bobbie-Lou, and me. Outside of going to church, we stayed at home most of the time. One of our favorite pastimes was listening to the radio programs popular during the 1940's: *Suspense, Boston Blackie, Jack Benny,*

Edgar Bergan and Charlie McCarthy, The F.B.I. in Peace and War, The Shadow, and many others.

Even though we had become a closer-knit family, there were still the little squabbles, especially since my father was still drinking and spending money foolishly.

Throughout this time God was also making changes in my own life.

I was in the habit of stealing from my Dad. From time-to-time, when Dad failed to come home when we expected him, Mom would take me downtown to look for him. He was usually in one of his favorite bars, and I had to go in to get him. My Dad was a happy drunk, and I would see him buy everyone drinks. I can remember Mom talking to him about the money he was spending, and I guess that's where I got the idea of stealing money out of his wallet. No one ever caught me.

Edison school didn't have a cafeteria so I would take the stolen money and go to the drug store lunch counter to buy whatever I wanted.

However, one day as I sat at the lunch counter with a twenty-dollar bill I had stolen from my father's wallet, I found I couldn't spend it. I was under conviction. I knew I had to quit stealing from my Dad, and I knew I had to put the money back, but how?

I lost my appetite that day. The twenty-dollar bill grew heavier and heavier in my pocket, and I grew more and more miserable. I was Student Council President. What would my friends think of me if they ever found out I was a thief? What would my mother think of me? What would my father think of me? What about the kids at Church? I had to think of a way to put the money back. Finally, I decided what I was going to do.

That same night, after my Dad had gone to bed and had fallen asleep; and after I could hear his snores, I crept into his room. Tip-toeing around the end of his bed to the closet, I reached for his wallet. I was hardly breathing, and my heart pounded so loudly in my chest that I prayed that the noise wouldn't awaken my Dad.

Fumbling around in his pants pocket, I slipped out his billfold. Carefully, I replaced that heavy twenty-dollar bill, put the billfold back into his pants pocket, and slipped silently out of the room. The weight of guilt was gone. I never stole from my Dad again. That was also the year my Dad quit drinking.

For years Dad continued happily drinking his way through life and spending money carelessly, until one evening, as he sat in boozy happiness in the kitchen, my mother decided that she had had enough. From his collection of fiddles, banjos, guitars, and mandolins, she grabbed his best fiddle, raised it high with both hands and with all her strength smashed it down on his head.

"Bob," she scolded. "You quit drinkin', or I'm outta here! Period! And I mean now!"

My father knew my Mom was serious. Shortly after, she took him to the Greyhound depot and put him on a bus for the rehabilitation center in Compton, California – but not before she plucked a half-pint of booze from his boot as he prepared to board the bus. My Dad returned home from Compton after almost seven weeks. He never drank again.

My Mom and Dad about 1951

I graduated from eighth-grade in 1952 at the age of fifteen. The summer following, I went to Church-camp in Granite Dells, Prescott. As the week went on and the daily speaker explained various aspects of the Gospel and the responsibilities of the believer in living a testimony, I began to wonder if I was really saved. I wanted to be certain that I was going to heaven. Finally, when the speaker gave the invitation, I went forward and rededicated my life to the Lord.

After returning home from church-camp, I spent a lot of time with my friends Ted, Red, Walter, and my brother, Bill. One day we decided to go swimming at the Salt River, right near the bridge at Canyon Lake. We found a place near the bridge where the water was about twenty-feet deep. There was a ledge and a cliff, and we decided to jump from there. Red and I climbed up to the ledge where he decided to jump. Foolishly, I decided to continue on to the top of the cliff. I was hot, sweaty and tired by the time I reached the top and stepped out onto the edge of the cliff. Looking down at the water about a hundred feet below, I glanced over at the bridge. It looked like a tinker-toy. I knew I was way too high to jump, but it was too hot to stay up there, and I was too beat to climb back down again. Besides, I was with Ted and Red, and I didn't want them to think I was "chicken."

I took a deep breath and leaped as far out as I could in order to miss the ledge from which Red had jumped. When I hit the water, I was in the wrong position, and it was like hitting a cement sidewalk. My left leg hit first to take all the force of the hundred-foot drop. I felt something like a million needles penetrating my body. I couldn't move. I went way down deep. I thought I was going to die. When I finally surfaced, Red and Ted were there. They grabbed me by the hair on my head and dragged me onto an inner tube to float me to shore. For a little while, I couldn't move my legs.

I was in pain for three weeks. Finally, after experiencing severe headaches, dizzy spells, and back pain, I went to see Dr. Van Dyke, an osteopath who was a member of our church. Dr. Van Dyke's daughter, Rhonda Kay Van Dyke, in later years became Miss America, 1966. Dr. Van Dyke discovered that the blow from my landing on the water the way I did had pushed my left leg back up into my hip and it was now two-inches shorter than my right leg. He had me stretch out on the table, and with a few twists and crunches, he set my leg back to where it belonged, I could walk again, and the pain went away. After a few days I was back to normal, but additional pain was ahead. Toward the end of the summer, I developed an agonizing ear infection and had to miss my first month at Phoenix Union High School.

Decisions

High School

In October of 1952, and over fifteen years old, I finally entered ninth grade at Phoenix Union High School. I was overwhelmed. Because of my ear-infection, I was behind all the other students who had been in school a month already; and they knew their way around. I was lost. Always having gone to small schools, I felt drowned in an ocean of 7,000 students swirling around me. Carrying my Bible and searching for classes in a huge, unfamiliar building, all I wanted to do was to get out of there. That's exactly what I decided to do. I would quit school.

I was old enough to quit. I had a motor-scooter to get around with, and having had part-time jobs of one kind or another, I knew how to work. I had learned how to drive. My Dad had his own trucking business that was doing well, and he had only a second-grade education. If he could do well with a second-grade education, I could do as well or better with an eighth-grade education. I could always work for my Dad to get started.

When I told my Dad of my decision, he was tickled. Even though he read only with the greatest difficulty with his limited education, he had worked hard and had built a successful business with several trucks and employees. He saw no problem with my succeeding, even if I did drop out of school.

With my mother, it was a different story.

"Son, she said. "You're a freshman. Your brain's not even finished growing. At least you gotta finish your education."

"Aw, Ma," I started to protest; but to argue with my mother was useless. With my father having been a drunk, she was the "Alpha" person in our house.

That Sunday I told my story to my friends in our church's young peoples' group. Most of them were students at Phoenix Christian High School, and one of the girls, Gloria Dodd, asked if I had thought about going there. I answered, "No."

The thought of going to a school like Christian High frightened me. I was a new Christian. I might not be "spiritual enough" to go there. In addition, I didn't think I was smart enough. What if I made a fool of myself in front of all my friends? I had no idea what a school like Christian High was like.

On the other hand, over twenty members of our young peoples' group were students at Christian High.

At least I would have friends there. Also, with only 265 students, it wasn't huge like Phoenix Union with its 7,000 students. Even some Christian High teachers were members of our church.

I decided to ask Pastor Garig about Christian High. He said, "Go."

I went home and spoke to my mother. She was all for it, but my father didn't agree. He said, "Don't go."

Finally, I decided to stay in school, and I enrolled in Phoenix Christian High School.

I had always had a part time job at A&S Gravel during the school year, and often I worked full-time during the summer parking cars. As a result, I had saved a good deal of money. Not needing to cash my paychecks from A&S, I had stuffed them in a jar in my room. Finally, the bookkeeper at A&S stopped me one day and asked, "Danny, where are your paychecks?"

"Well," I replied, "I'm waiting until school starts, and then I'll cash them."

"Don't you know that if this company went broke, you would lose all your money?" she said.

I went home, emptied the jar of all my checks, took them to the bank, and came home with my cash. After that, I always cashed my checks.

As soon as I could, cash in hand, I registered at Christian High and started classes.

The first time I walked on campus, I knew that this was where I belonged. At close to sixteen, I was the oldest student in the freshman class.

During my years at Christian High, I always had some kind of part-time job. One well-paying job was parking cars at Durant's, a high-end restaurant on Central Avenue. Many celebrities ate there, and they tipped generously. That income supplied enough money for my tuition with some left over. My second year at Christian High, I used some of the extra money to help out one of my best friends, Ted Stubbs, by paying his tuition.

I had to be careful about that. Ted had a strong sense of self-respect, and he resented anyone doing anything for him. His family had moved from Alabama to Phoenix and had rented a house around the corner from us.

We got to know the Stubbs family well, and we loved them all. My Mom especially loved Ted's mother's southern accent. We soon discovered the Stubbs was a family in crisis. Ted's father was a violent drunk – so violent that young Ted would sleep with a knife under his pillow for fear his father would harm him. Eventually the father deserted the family, and Ted's mother struggled to keep the family together and to put food on the table.

Ted would have been deeply hurt if he had known at that time that I had paid his tuition. He was very sensitive about his lack of finances to the point that he wouldn't let anyone buy him even a milkshake. One day, I watched him take a milkshake someone else had bought for him and pour it out on the street. In spite of that sensitivity, he had a curious contradiction. It didn't seem to occur to him to look for an after-school job to help out with family finances or to save for next-year's tuition. I never told him that I had paid his way. However, thirty years later, his mom told him.

Because I was older than my classmates, I was able to succeed in many areas, especially in sports. In my freshman year, I lettered as a varsity pole-vaulter. The next year, after having lost only one game, PCHS won the State championship in football in our division. I went on to letter in basketball, track and football. In the course of my four years at Phoenix Christian High School, I was the first student to letter in four times in three different sports.

The years I spent at Christian High were a wonderful time in my life. That I gave up the thought of quitting school and choosing to go to Christian High was one of the best decisions I have ever made in my life.

My Senior picture, 1956

Then one great dark time came. My Mom, who worked in the kitchen at the school, died from cancer when I was in my senior year.

Everything happened rapidly. Having persistent intestinal pain that increased as time went on, my mother thought it was the same kind of thing she had been taking medication for over the last several years. When the stomach medication stopped working, she went to the Doctor who believed her problem was gallstones. She was admitted into the hospital and went into surgery. When the surgeons started to operate, they found advanced and inoperable cancer. They stopped operating and closed the incision. When she recovered, the Doctor gave her the news that she had only about three months to live.

I was working at my Saturday part-time job at A&S Gravel when my boss told me I was needed at home. I felt that was strange, and I could tell by the quiver in his voice that something was wrong. I got into my 1936 four-door Ford sedan and started for the Garfield house. When I arrived home, my brother, Bill was there with my Aunt Effie. She told me the doctors had discovered my mom had cancer and that it was too far advanced for them to operate. She had only ninety days to live. I had a hard time handling that news. Mom was the glue that held everything together in our home. I didn't know how we would be able to get along without her.

I went to the hospital to see my mom, and it was a teary visit. We had a heart-rending conversation. One of the things we talked about was my brother Bill. She said something was wrong with Bill and that I would have to look out after him. We didn't know it then, but my brother had schizophrenia.

Billy Henderson, April 1953

My mom died on January 6, 1956, and over 250 people packed the First Missionary Church for her funeral. My father took my mother's death hard. I think he began to realize that he had taken her too much for granted. He was crushed, lost his enthusiasm and energy, and had bouts of depression.

During my final semester at Phoenix Christian, school and work helped me keep my mind off the loss of my mother. After graduation on May 14, 1956, I went to work for A&S Gravel full-time.

In my free time, I hung out with my friends, and one weekend, Jim Patterson, Ted and Dwight Stubbs, Walt Ageney, and I decided to take a trip up north. We went to Granite Dells where our denomination had a church camp. I don't remember why and how, but Dwight and Walt got into a fight with some drunk guys. After that, we decided to go to the Grand Canyon. We ate breakfast at the Bright Angel Lodge. The restaurant was packed. After we finished eating, Ted took out a firecracker. I knew what he was planning.

I had a bum leg from a bad landing in the pole-vault pit, and I could barely walk. I told Ted to wait until I got a head start to get to the car. Ted nodded his head and started taking the gunpowder out of the fuse. I got my head start, but it didn't help much.   When Ted lit the firecracker it went off a lot sooner than he expected. People dropped oatmeal, grapefruit, forks, coffee and glared at us as we all hurried out of the restaurant.

Piling into the car, we took off along the canyon access road. Someone looked back and saw three guys in a car following us. We pulled over and got out at a sightseeing pull-out, and the three guys in the car turned in and stopped behind us. When they saw there were five of us and only three of them, and they turned around and left.

While we were at the pull-out we saw a porcupine up in a tree. Dwight picked up a large branch to knock the porcupine off the branch where it was clinging, but as he draw back to hit the porcupine, he hit Walt in the head and almost knocked him out. Walt yelled out in pain, and the porcupine got away. I wasn't happy that Walt got hit, but I was happy the porcupine got away.

Toward the end of that long, blistering summer, I worked on road construction. The asphalt I had to spread came off the truck at 200 degrees, and the sun seared the Valley throughout the summer months through August when the temperature reached 115 degrees. That's when I decided I didn't want to shovel and spread asphalt the rest of my life. The thought of cool and comfortable college classrooms grew more and more appealing.

After high school, many of my PCHS friends had gone on to college. Having worked at various jobs since I was a child, and coming from a family of blue-collar workers, I wasn't overly interested in academics or college. I had done well in high school, but college hadn't been particularly high in my plans. However, the more I thought about long, searing, sweaty summers and going home to scrub the stink and grit of black asphalt off my body, I changed plans and decided to go to Fort Wayne Bible College. That's where the other kids at our church went.

When my shift ended, I left the pile of asphalt, drove home, and got cleaned up.

Ted's house was only a block away, so I walked over to see him and found him sitting out on the front porch.

"Hey, Ted," I said, "I'm sick of doin' this asphalt. Let's get educated. Let's go to Fort Wayne."

"You gotta be crazy," Ted grunted.

Red Angerney lived nearby. We all went to the same church, and Red knew Fort Wayne was the main college of our denomination. I decided to give him a try. Leaving Ted I made my way over to Red's house.

"Hey, Red," I said, "Let's go to college."

"Sounds like a good idea to me," Red replied.

By now, I had gone through and gotten rid of my 1936 Ford and 1939 Ford Convertible I had driven through high school. Toward the end of August, 1957, my dad gave me $200 and his old 1948 Dodge pickup, and Red and I were on our way to Fort Wayne, Indiana.

College

When Red and I got to Fort Wayne Bible College, we were met by the dean, and he asked why we thought we should be accepted. We told him we were both born-again Christians. Red had graduated high school in three years and was a straight "A" student, and I had graduated with a "B" average. Those were the days before having to submit transcripts and all sorts of other documents. We were admitted.

Leaving the Dean's office, we made our way across campus to our dormitory. Thick green grass and green-leaved trees seemed to be everywhere. Brought up in the greys and browns of the Sonoran desert where everything stuck, poked, and bit, we couldn't get over the soft lushness. Added to that was the coolness of the Indiana air. Red and I felt as though we were in a different world. "Some change from triple digit Phoenix heat," we thought. We found the dormitory building, located our room, and moved in.

As much as I enjoyed my new surroundings, I was poorly prepared for the demands of college life. I struggled with my classes and with the time I had to put in outside of class to study. When they told me I had to put in two hours of study time for each hour spent in class, my heart sank because I had signed up for too many credit hours and had to work full-time. I couldn't keep up.

Because both Red and I had found full-time jobs, we couldn't get involved with most of the social life at college. We had entered as a couple of "outsiders" dressed in "T" shirts and Levi's. Fort Wayne was a "shirt and tie" campus. For the year we were there, we pretty much remained outsiders.

Red got a job at a carpenter shop, and I found a job at a Standard Gas Station. Indiana in the fall didn't bother us "desert transplants." Even when it got to Thanksgiving, when Red and I hitch-hiked home, the cold was no worse than a Phoenix winter.

After the Thanksgiving break, when we got back to school, it was a different story. Indiana was in the grip of a record cold winter. Fortunately, someone in our church had given me a warm overcoat. Even though I made full use of it and added every sweater I had underneath it, I was always cold.

Since Mom had died, I was concerned about how things were going at home; and I decided to go back to

Phoenix on Christmas break. When time for Christmas break arrived, Red and I were too broke to afford to drive my truck back to Phoenix. We had some friends at Wheaton College in Glen Ellyn, Illinois, and they told us we could leave my truck there. We decided to do that and hitch-hike back to Phoenix. In those days, people were much more willing to pick up a couple of college guys and give them a lift.

Arriving back home, I was in for a shock. There were only three people left living in the Garfield house: my brother, Bill, my Dad – and Rosa! My father had gotten married while I was away at school. That angered me. I couldn't accept that he had married so soon after my mother's death. I didn't like Rosa, and she didn't like me.

My Dad married Rosa while I was at college
My Dad is in the middle, Pastor Gerig on the left,
and Rosa.

There was a lot of tension, and it was not a happy Christmas. I was glad to leave and get back to school

Red and I hitch-hiked our way back to Glen Ellyn to pick up my truck. The closer we got to Wheaton, the colder it became. We wanted to get that trip over with. When we reached my truck, we were eager to get started. The truck offered no comfort. It was an old, stripped down vehicle my Dad had bought after the war. It had no radio and, more importantly, no heater. We couldn't start back for Fort Wayne soon enough. Even back then, the roads and streets in the Chicago suburbs were a spider-web of confusion. We discovered that the hard way. After a freezing two hours or so, we saw a sign for Champaign, Illinois and discovered we had gone a hundred miles in the wrong direction. Turning around, we pointed that old, cold Dodge back toward Wheaton. We had never been so cold in our lives; but many hours later, we finally made it back to Fort Wayne and the warmth of our dormitory room.

Finally, the winter ended, and Spring came with its rain and mud. In May, 1958, with its sunshine and greenery, the school year ended.   Red and I were both ready to go home. I sold my pickup, bought a 1948 Ford Club Coupe, and we drove back to Phoenix. At least the

Coupe had a radio – and if we ever needed one, a heater.

Changes

The Chest

When I arrived home, I was shocked at the changes. I had already discovered at Christmas time that my Dad had married Rosa, and I still had trouble dealing with that; but I had a feeling that something more was wrong. Deciding to keep an eye on things, I moved in with my father and his wife and found a job at a Shell Gas Station.

My feelings about my father marrying so soon after my mother's death became obvious; and it didn't take long for tensions to develop between me and Rosa. With my father caught in the middle, and not knowing how to respond, the tensions stretched to a breaking point.

Then I noticed something that really blew the lid off. Years before, during the Second World War, a Japanese family had left the cedar chest with us in our house. They had never returned to claim it. Over the years we had used it as a "catch-all" to store various odds and ends. What I noticed now was that there was a new hasp attached, and the hasp was secured with a padlock. Nothing in our house had ever before been locked. Suspicious, I went to where my father kept his tools and dug out a pair of bolt-cutters. By now, my father was with me. Returning to the living-room, I snapped the lock with the bolt-cutter and opened the chest.

Inside the chest I found documents showing that my Dad had sold his business, "Bob's Transfer" to Atlas Van Lines for $30,000. Beneath those papers were the war-bonds my parents had accumulated through the war years. They had all matured. I examined them more closely and discovered that my father's new wife,

Rosa, had talked my Dad into making them payable to Rosa "or" Robert Henderson, not Rosa "and" Robert Henderson. I looked up at my father.

"What in the world, Dad," I asked, "is this all about?"

"It's all right," my father replied, "Rosa told me we both had to sign the bonds."

Having gone only to the second-grade in school, my father didn't realize the word "or" instead of "and" would enable Rosa alone to cash the bonds. Rosa obviously intended to rob my father and cash out the bonds for herself.

I didn't waste any time. I got Dad into my car and drove him to the bank. Once there, I had him sign and cash in the bonds. He didn't realize how much the bonds were worth. When it finally hit him how close he had come to losing all that money, his knees were so wobbly, he could hardly walk.

He suddenly realized that Rosa had married him only for his money. In their five months together, she had manipulated him into signing the bonds and into signing over half the proceeds from the sale of his business. She used the old line, ". . . If you love me, you would trust me."

Later that day, Rosa came home to see the cedar chest with its sheared padlock lying on the floor in front of it. She knew she had been found out. It was over.

When she learned it was I who had discovered her schemes, she became livid and screamed, "Kiss my ass, Danny!"

"Mark the spot, 'cause you're all ass to me," I replied. I was always pretty proud of that response.

Although we were able to save all of the bonds from her grasp, Rosa got to keep her half of the proceeds from the sale of my Dad's business. With no more money to steal from my father, she left him shortly after.

There were other tensions that surfaced as I lived at home that summer and fall. Bill, my younger brother continued to suffer from Schizophrenia. With my mother gone – she had been the one to keep things calm -- and with the turmoil with Rosa, my father was overwhelmed. He couldn't handle Bill.

In the 1950's there were few effective treatments for Bill's condition, and he had gotten worse over the months since my mother's death.

I didn't realize how bad the situation had become until one afternoon when I came home from work and heard my brother yelling and screaming out in the back yard.

"I can't do anything with him," my father said. "Go out back and beat him up."

I seethed with anger. All my life, I had never been allowed to touch Bill. No matter how bad it got, he was always the protected one because he was "sick." Now my Dad sticks me with this?

"What a low-class thing," I fumed inside. "Dad makes me go out and handle Bill."

I stalked out back, and even though Bill was bigger, I tore into him. I don't remember how long our fight lasted, but it got so loud that the neighbors called the police to come to break us up. The police arrived, pulled us apart, handcuffed us, and put us in the back of a "Paddy Wagon." They kept us long enough to get us calmed down, then removed the cuffs and let us go.

I was still fuming, not at my brother, but at my father. Never before, or after, was I so disappointed in him. My anger lived like a cold, hard lump in my heart until the day before my Dad died.

After Rosa left, my father, my brother, Bill, and I all lived together in the same house. Summer came to an end, and I decided to give school another try. I wanted to keep my job at the Shell station, so when I enrolled at Phoenix College, I chose a much lighter course load.

I fell into the routine of school, of work, and of coming home to clean up and eat supper. Phoenix College wasn't the challenge that Fort Wayne was. Over the next few months, I had various part-time jobs. One of the first was that of selling Kirby vacuum cleaners. I enjoyed the incentives. After I sold eight vacuum cleaners, I would get a free vacuum cleaner to sell, and I could keep all the money for myself. Additional incentives included free dinners at the Green Gables Restaurant. A hallmark of that restaurant was the Tudor-style building. Out in front of the building, and seated in a live horse was a man decked out in full armor like a real knight.

Although selling Kirby vacuum cleaners was easy work, and I made some money, my sales withered away after I ran out of friends whom I could talk into feeling the need for a new vacuum cleaner. I found another job pumping gas at a Shell station.

With a part-time job to put a little money in my pocket, and with a light load at college, I had free time. By now I had sold the 1948 coupe to Red and had bought a 1949 brown Ford convertible. It was perfect for "cruising Central" and looking for pretty girls. That's how we met Diane and Donna.

Top down and cruising slowly in the curb lane, we spotted them walking along on the sidewalk. My friend, Ted, and I frequently joined the Saturday night cruisers flowing up and down Central. In my Ford convertible we pulled up alongside the girls and started chatting. Diane was pretty enough, but Ted and I both had eyes for Donna.

"Wanna go get a Coke?" we asked.

"Okay," they said.

Over the next three weeks we all went out together a couple or three times.

I was almost twenty-one, and as a Christian, I had decided not to have sex until I got married. One evening, about a month later, I drove up in front of Diane's house to drop her off. On an impulse, I said to her, "Let's go to Mexico and get married."

I thought I was joking.

Diane didn't.

She hopped out of the car, went into the house, and came out again with her bag. She slid back into the seat beside me. I put that old 1948 Ford convertible into gear, and we headed to Nogales and marriage.

When we got Nogales, I discovered no one could speak English. Finally, we found a little boy who could understand and translate for us. When he discovered we were there to get married, he nodded and led us to a rundown building.   I guessed it must have housed the office of something like a Justice of the Peace, or whatever they called it in Mexico. He led us up a flight of old creaking stairs.

By now, I was more than nervous. This was downright creepy. When we entered the room at the top of the stairs, we faced an official-looking person. With the boy acting as translator, we stated our business. Then we discovered, through translation, that we couldn't get married legally unless we had a blood test first. At that point I came to my senses and said, "No. This isn't legal." We left the office, went back down those creaky stairs, got back in the car, turned around, and drove back home.

I didn't go back to Phoenix College. Actually, I didn't even bother finishing the first semester. College just wasn't for me. I decided to go back to work. With college no longer in my plans, I sold my 1949 Ford and bought a 1956 Ford Victoria..

Marriage

When I told my father I was getting married, he was very disappointed and spoke against it. He said I was, "too young," and "too impulsive." He had hopes that I would join him to build the business up and eventually take it over. That I would be getting married was a big jolt to him and a great disappointment. After Mom had died, having to deal with the fact of my getting married, and that there would be no one to take over the business, probably started to take away my Dad's hopes for the future of the business he had worked all his life to build.

On Valentine's Day, 1958, with Red standing in as my best man, Diana and I got married in the First Missionary Church. About 250 people came. Following tradition, Ted, Red and his friends decided to paint all kinds of messages on my recently-purchased 1956 Ford. What I discovered later was that they had used shoe-polish to complete that prank. When I tried to remove the "Just Married" messages, the shoe-polish refused to come off, no matter what I used. I ended up repainting my car. I was not happy about that.

Diana's mother, one sister and four younger brothers accepted and liked me. They lived together in a house that was a little more than they could really afford, and they all had to work to make the monthly payments. There was no money to spare. All the girls were eager to move out and get married. That's when I suddenly understood Diane's ready acceptance of my marriage proposal.

Diane's family was largely unchurched, and when they did go to church, it was only occasionally to an Episcopalian church. I had spoken to Diane about religion, and she had agreed to speak to my pastor. She went to see him, and when she came back she said she'd, "got converted." Later, I would wonder about that.

For the few months after we got married, Diane and I lived in a covered motor home in back of my father's house. He had placed it there years before as a sort of "guest house," and a number of our family had used it. Now it was my turn. After a couple of months, I was earning enough money by setting pool tile for Leroy Fairey, and I was able to rent a little house on 12th Street and Portland.

After Diane and I moved off the Garfield property, my sister, Bobby-Lou, with her five children, moved into the Garfield house to live with my father and Billy. Bobby-Lou had separated from her husband years before. A member of the Holiness Church, she didn't believe in divorce, so she and her husband had remained separated the rest of their lives.

By now, with my job working for Leroy, I was learning more and more about building pools. As I learned how the business worked, Leroy gave me more and more responsibility. In addition, I got to be known around the industry and was well-liked. Diane was pregnant with our first child, and things were going well. Then, during the summer of 1958, my life took an unexpected turn.

On my way to work in my Ford Victoria, I rear-ended another car. I had no insurance, and it didn't take long to find out that the other driver was planning to sue me.

Pretty close to broke, I figured the wisest thing to do would be to leave town.

I had a little money saved so I gave Leroy my notice, explained my reasons, packed up Diane, pregnant at this time; and we headed for San Diego..

My sister, Imogene, lived in Chula Vista and worked for Rohr Aircraft. I figured I could get a job there. I was wrong. When I applied, they told me that there would be heavy lifting involved, and because I had hurt my back in my swimming accident, they didn't want to take a chance on hiring me.

On February 25, 1959, a month after we arrived in San Diego, Danny Mark was born.

With new responsibilities, I had to find work. With my experience in the pool industry in Phoenix, I was soon able to get some part-time jobs with various pool companies. That helped us scrape by until I got hired on with the San Diego Police Department. After finishing the academy, I discovered I really liked the work and even started thinking about of making a career of it. The pay was good; I would be able to support a family. I even thought that, in time, I might even become a detective. Every day I could hardly wait to put on my gear, pin on my badge, and go.

But Diane hated my being in police work. We stayed only nine months in San Diego. I decided to listen to my wife and quit the police force. In early December, 1960, we packed up our belongings in a U-Haul trailer and headed back to Phoenix.

During the months we were in San Diego, I hadn't had much contact with my family back in Phoenix, and I doubted they had even realized I had moved away. I began to wonder if they even cared.

I had seen my father briefly on a short visit the month before, and he seemed okay, but it was obvious to me that he had been going downhill ever since my mother had died. With his failed second marriage to Rosa, the disappointment and stress of how she had tried to take advantage of him, and the family chaos – I think he finally just gave up.

After we arrived back in Phoenix, we unpacked, and I found a job with Ray Pools. When I finally went to see my father, I was shocked. His body had wasted away to little more than skin and bones. His cheeks were sunken. His eyes were black and there was little life left in them. Seeing him like this drained the last drop of the festering anger I had been harboring toward him.

Bobbie Lou told me that my father had eaten little over the last month, and he had seldom gotten out of bed.

I picked him up to put him in my car and take him to County hospital at 35th Avenue and Durango. I was surprised at how light he was. He died the next day, December 6, 1960.

My Father's funeral service, like my mother's was held at the First Missionary Church, but fewer people attended – only about 150. My four older sisters came from various parts of the country as well as various aunts and uncles.

Settling the estate was a straightforward affair. We gave Bobbie Lou the house she was living in, and then we sold the rentals. We sold the bonds and the half business interest that he had left from the "Rosa" debacle. With everything converted to cash, we divided the money equally. When all was settled, we each received $5,000. With my share, I gave Red and Donna enough for a down payment on a house. Choosing lots close to each other, we bought new Hallcraft homes for $10,000 each. Our house payment came to seventy-four dollars a month.

I thought I was set. I had a wife. I had money. I had a house, and I had a job. Then I had a car wreck.

In 1959 I had worked for Ray pools for only a short time before leaving town for San Diego. After I returned to Phoenix, Leroy Fairey hired me back where my friend, Ted, also worked. Living close to one another, we often shared rides in our commute to work. One morning as I rode to work with Ted in his new Austin-Healey, at the intersection of 16th Street and Missouri Avenue, a full-sized Buick Roadmaster turned left in front of us. We hit it head-on.

When I awoke in the hospital, I had no memory of the collision. Those were the days before seatbelts, and my head had gone through the windshield. In addition, I had broken my back and had ended up lying unconscious in the street. Ted had also been hurt, and he'd had several of his front teeth knocked out.

Suddenly, I was out of work, and I was unable to return for almost a year. Fortunately, I had saved a little money, and I still had a little left from my inheritance. In addition, Diane had found work at the phone company. 1960 was a lean and mean year, but I healed faster than expected and was able to return to work in April of 1961, and we survived.

The Pool

Floater

Working for Leroy before my accident, I not only had set tile, but also I had learned how to build a complete swimming pool. Diane and I already had Danny. By the time our second child, Lois, was about a year old, there was another child, Debbie, already on the way. I decided to build a swimming pool for my kids.

Confident I had the skills to build the pool myself. I drew up the plans for a ten-foot by forty-foot diving pool. It would be ten feet deep and one end and three-and-a-half feet deep at the other.

The accident in Ted's car had brought my plans to an abrupt stop for a short time, but when I had healed enough to supervise, I contracted out the steel, the gunite, and the plumbing. The plumbing was a little fussy because I had to reroute my sewer line all the way to the alley where the city had to come in with a backhoe to dig a deep trench to reconnect it to the city's main line.

Building that pool took nine months, from January to September 1961. By then I was pretty much healed up from my broken back, and when I looked at the completed shell, I sighed a big sigh of relief -- both for the pool and for my healed body.

I decided that I deserved a little reward. Dove season was coming up, and it had been a long time since I had the feel of a shotgun in my hands. I got in touch with Red and Ted and set a day to go dove-hunting in Buckeye.

I had been a hunter almost as soon as I could walk. We'd always had guns in the house when I was growing up, and almost as soon as I could walk and hold one, my father was careful to teach me to how to handle guns safely. When I was fourteen, I got my first gun, a .410 shotgun, and after school, my friends and I would often go plinking down at the Salt River bottom. "Yes," I thought, "It'll be good to make my 12 gauge go "bang" and feel the recoil again."

When I picked up Ted and Red in the morning of our outing, the sky was overcast with heavy grey clouds. We figured we would get a little rain, but rain, though it could be intense, seldom lasted long in the desert. During the forty-minute drive to Buckeye, the rain started, but it wasn't enough to interfere with our shooting. We arrived at our site, and during the next several hours, we each bagged our limit. We started home at mid-afternoon and, as we approached Phoenix, it became obvious that it had rained much harder there.

I dropped off Ted and Red and headed home. Turning into my driveway, I immediately saw that something was very, very, wrong. Blue and white coping extended several feet above the six-foot fence bordering my back yard. I blinked. This had to be a bad dream. Could this really be happening? It was no dream. My empty pool shell had floated up and out of the ground; and the deep end was up about eight feet. Why was my pool floating like a big concrete boat?

While my friends and I hunted out in Buckeye, Phoenix had experienced far more rain than where we were. Situated at the low end of a tract of houses, my home had received all of the run-off from the storm. Because of the size and shape of my pool, several weeks earlier the city had to dig deep in the alley to accommodate my rerouted sewer line. When the city backfilled the trench, they failed to compact it properly. As a result, the runoff, instead of remaining on the surface and continuing on down the alley, it simply seeped through the backfill to form a reservoir which migrated over into the hole I had excavated for my pool. The runoff filled the hole like a big bathtub, and it floated my pool right out of the ground.

What do I do with a floating pool? All my experience with Ray pools had not prepared me for this.

It hadn't prepared Diane, either. As the pool had started its ominous rise from its cavity in the ground, Diane stood staring through the glass of the patio door and moaning, "My house is sinking. My house is sinking."

My kids playing by my "floating pool."

As the neighbors became aware of my floating pool, it became a sight-seeing attraction. Before long, a reporter from the *Arizona Republic* showed up to photograph my concrete catastrophe. The next day, my concrete boat was pictured on the front page of the morning edition of the paper under the headline, "Ever See a Floating Swimming Pool?"

For two days I stared at the pool and tried to decide what to do. I thought the most logical approach would be to knock a hole in the bottom of the shell to let the water flow back in. I believed the pool would then settle back into its original place. Grabbing my sledge-hammer, I went at it. It didn't work. When the water level inside the pool equaled the water level outside the pool, it stopped sinking and settled about three feet above the grade. I was stuck.

For almost a month I struggled at least to level the pool, but nothing worked. Finally, I decided to give up on the "floater," to tear the whole thing out, and to start again from scratch.

Before I got out my sixteen-pound sledge-hammer, I had one last idea to avoid having to demolish the pool. I called Arizona House Movers. I figured that if they could move the pool in one piece, then I could start again from the original excavation and save an unbelievable amount of work. When the house-moving company learned the size of the pool, however, they told me the pool was too wide, and they would be unable to get it down the alley. I had no choices left. It was up to me and my hammer. I would have to demolish the pool by hand.

I swung my sixteen-pound sledge for over eighteen months. Every afternoon after work and on weekends I whacked away on that concrete. In the heat of the summer, I would wait until sunset before I would start swinging my hammer. When I had loosened up enough chunks of concrete to fill the bed of my truck, I'd haul it off to the dump and then come back to start all over again. I lost count of how many pairs of leather gloves I wore out, and in spite of the gloves, my hands grew raw. Demolishing that pool was excruciating work, and I had to live with repeated and sudden muscle spasms. Little by little I nibbled away at that concrete shell. My fences were down, and I became a sort of local sight-seeing attraction as my neighbors and others would stop by to view my progress. One of my neighbors later told me, "Many nights I fell asleep to the rhythmic beat of Danny and his sledge-hammer."

At last, after a year-and-a-half, and after all my effort, I could gaze at nothing more than a huge rectangular hole in the ground. No more trips to the dump with a tuck full of rubble. No more swinging that sledge hour after hour. No more shredded leather gloves and raw hands. Finally, I could start on my new pool. One big plus that I could enjoy emerged from this whole catastrophe was that I had learned far more about how to build a swimming pool than I could ever have learned simply by working for someone else. The knowledge and the skills I developed in the building and tearing out of my pool contributed to my success in future ventures.

Now it was time to fill that hole in the ground with a brand-new pool – one that wouldn't float. Having learned much from my recent disaster about providing sufficient drainage beneath a pool, I filled fifteen-hundred cement sacks with gravel and lined the sides of the hole. I followed that with forming the cement shell inside of the lined hole. From the old pool, I reused the same filter, steel, plumbing, tile, coping, and flagstone. At last my new dogleg pool was complete.

Lining the sides of the hole with sacks filled with gravel

I supervised workers on my new pool.

Friends

Ted

All through 1960 and to 1961, the fallout from the accident in which Ted and I were injured, consumed months of litigation; but finally it appeared that the end was in sight.

Because the other driver in the collision had no insurance, outside of what his own insurance covered, Ted received no additional money. As a result, he engaged a lawyer to go after the other driver. Ted's lawyer told him that I would have the best chance of winning in the event of a lawsuit, especially since I was out of work with a broken back and that I may have to change professions.

When I spoke with Ted's attorney, he assured me that I indeed had a good chance of winning a lawsuit, and since I was out of work, the chance of a $10,000 lawsuit split equally between Ted and me sounded pretty good.

However, during the two years while the back and forth of the litigation lasted, my back was healing. In mid-1961, when it came time for me to give a final deposition for Ted's insurance company to settle, I was pretty much back to normal and was already back at work, this time in Las Vegas where I was preparing to move my family.

In spite of fact that I was fully back to normal and carrying a full work load, the lawyer urged me to claim that my back was still hurting.

I refused. "No," I said. "I'm not going to lie in court."

The attorney was livid, telling me how hard he had worked on my case and how much time and effort and money he had spent getting this settlement and getting ready for court.

I told him that the only reason I agreed to sue was that I was concerned about my back. Now that my back was healed, I didn't want to go to court..

We finally came to an agreement. I told him to settle for his fees, and if he got more than his fees, to send the extra to First Missionary Church anonymously. That was how we left it. I never got a dime, but I had recovered. Thank the Lord!

When I told Ted what I had done, he didn't believe me. He was convinced that I had gotten the $10,000 and that I was cheating him out of his share. I could not convince him that I had never accepted a dime from the settlement. Hurt and angry that he refused to believe me, I failed to resolve the matter.

As years went by, I always felt I should make the first move to reconcile with Ted, but I let it slide. As a result I allowed a treasured friendship from the time we were children to be destroyed. Many years later, when I learned that Ted was dying of terminal cancer, we came together. Both saddened by the fifteen years we had wasted, we mended our friendship. Ted died in 2006. I loved him, and I still miss him.

With tears, Ted and I restored our
lifelong friendship shortly before he died.

Ted's mother lived to the age of 103. She never lost that southern accent that my own mother loved to hear. His brother, Dwight, lived to be eighty, and his sister, Lois, and his other brother, Lee, still live here in Phoenix.

Pat

During this time, I had another friend, Pat Shaughnessy. He tells his own interesting story in detail in his book, *Headin' Home.* This is how I was involved.

I had started doing jobs for myself, and Pat Shaughnessy worked with me as my tile helper. He lived in our neighborhood and had begun going to our church because he wanted to play on our softball team. About that time he met his future wife, Jan, and fell madly in love with her. Not long after, Jan became pregnant. They married and moved into a house they rented from Jan's mom. Pat's mother-in-law didn't like Pat at that time.

As we worked together setting tile, Pat and I became friends.

One day, while Jan and Pat were eating supper at Jan's mother's house, there was a family blow up. The next day, when Pat and Jan arrived home with their infant child, their house was locked up. The mother-in-law, Jan's mother, had locked them out. Locked out of their home, they came over to my house. As they told me their story, I asked if the rent was paid. They said that it was paid until the end of the month.

Everything they owned, including the baby's stuff, was locked up inside their house. I told Pat, "Let's go and get the baby's diapers, bottles, and clothes."

Pat and I got into my truck and we drove over to Mesa where they lived. When we got to the front door we found it still locked. Pat said, "What are we going to do?"

I asked again, "Pat, is your rent paid up?"

He said, "Yes, I assure you the rent is paid."

I took a step forward and kicked the door open. Well, that was the wrong thing to do. Jan's mother was the secretary for the Chief of Police in Mesa. The next thing we knew, the police were there; and soon Pat and I were in handcuffs and on our way to the Mesa jail. I tried to figure out how to get out of this mess and decided to call Walter Arnold, the pickle man. His dad owned Arnold Pickle Company.

We were in jail for only a few hours when Walter's dad came to bail us out. We got a police escort back to their house and got some of their things. With no other place to live, Pat and Jan stayed with us for a few months.

I had been praying for Pat a long time. One evening, alone in my pickup, I had stopped at a red light on Seventh Street and Maryland Avenue. Sitting there waiting for the light to change, I heard a voice say to me, "You don't have to pray for Pat anymore because he is going to get saved next Sunday."

My burden for Pat lifted, and I could hardly wait for the next Sunday. When Sunday arrived, we were all at church. Our preacher, Bob Magary, didn't give an invitation that morning until his closing prayer. He stopped his closing prayer and said he felt the Holy Spirit was working in someone's heart. As he spoke those words, Pat and Jan walked down the aisle to accept Christ as their personal Savior. That morning many others in the congregation were born again. It was a joyous occasion.

To this day I still hear that heavenly voice predict Pat's salvation. Pat was on fire for the Lord. A few years later, he and his new family moved to Fort Wayne, Indiana where he attended Fort Wayne Bible College. Because he had to work to support his family while going to school, it took him six years to graduate.

During his senior year, Pat got a call from a little church back here in Phoenix. He accepted the call, and God blessed his ministry. Over the years Pat's ministry flourished and eventually grew to the largest church in our association.

Pat Shaughnessy (left). The church he served grew to become the largest in his denomination.

In 1973, Pat was invited to South Korea to preach. He was at the airline ticket counter in Los Angeles when an exploding bomb blew his leg off. The blast threw him through the air for about eighteen feet. He never lost consciousness, and when his ambulance got to the hospital, the driver opened the door and yelled for someone to give him a hand, not excuses. "I have a guy with both his legs blown off." Pat said that shout almost killed him. The person was wrong about both legs. Now on one leg and walking with a prosthesis, Pat has recovered and is still preaching God's Word.

The Arnolds

Nancy and Walter Arnold

Back in the early '70s, the Arnolds and their friends, the Aycocks and the Corkrans, came to Vegas to celebrate the New Year's holiday. However, they couldn't get rooms. They called me and asked if I could give them a hand. It just so happened I could.

From being in the pool business, I knew of two penthouse suites with leaking spas at Caesar's Palace. To work on them, we had blocked off two rooms. Since it was December 30th, we decided that the Aycocks and Corkrans and I would spend the night at Caesar's Palace. In the process of getting ready for a time of year-end celebration, we became a bit rowdy, but finally we went to bed. The next night was my birthday, and also it was New Year's Eve.

That night the Arnolds and Aycocks stayed in the same room as the night before. I cautioned Walter not to answer the door if anyone knocked on it, but if for any reason they were discovered, I emphasized, "Do not use my name."

The next morning, New Year's Day, my phone rang about 8:00 A.M., and Walter told me someone was knocking on their door. I told him, "Don't open the door." He said, "Okay," and hung up. About ten minutes later, Walter called me again. He said the same thing as before, but the knocking was getting more aggressive. Again, I said, "Don't open the door." Walter asked me if I was sure about not opening the door. I wasn't sure, but I said again, "Don't open the door." About a half-hour went by, and my phone rang again. It was Walter, and he said, "Danny, there's a security guard outside the window, and he is tapping on the window with his pistol." This time I said, "Open the door but don't mention my name because we do a lot of business with Caesar's."

The security guard had taken them all down to the front desk. They were questioned, but they didn't use my name. Eventually they were charged fifty dollars and told not to come back to Caesar's Palace. Although they never gave me up, the Arnolds and the Aycocks never let me live down that episode, and they always teased me about my helping friends with their hotel reservations.

Business

Marine Tile

By the middle of 1961, due to a strike by the cement workers and suppliers, the pool industry pretty much ground to a stop.

I had been working for Leroy Fairey with Joe Noble, a pool contractor with Leroy. Joe and I had apprenticed together at Perry Tile in the tile and coping area of the business.

In August, 1962 Joe took me with him to Las Vegas to work on the pools at the "Tally-Ho," a projected million-dollar 450 room motel. Built in the English Tudor-style, it had gabled roofs and leaded windows. The owners wanted to see if a hotel without a casino could survive in Las Vegas. They expected it would take two years to complete, and best of all, they had planned to build four large luxury swimming pools.

Las Vegas was just a small town then, and it had few pool contractors. Joe introduced me to some people he knew and then returned to Phoenix without me. I ended up staying and working in Las Vegas. I asked him later, "Joe, how come you took me up there?"

"You were my competition," he said. "I wanted to get rid of you."

It didn't take me long to realize I could make a living in Las Vegas; and in December, 1962, I got a contractor's license and named my new business "Marine Tile and Coping."

During this time, I had rented a house on Charleston and Campbell and had arranged to have a house built in preparation for bringing out my family. Diane and I put our house up for sale and I brought Diane and the family to Las Vegas in December of 1962

Vegas Move

By the time we went back to get the rest of our belongings in Phoenix, our house had sold. We owned a 1962 Chevrolet, and on Christmas Eve, we began pulling a trailer full of our things to Las Vegas. Twenty-five miles outside Kingman, Arizona, at 10:50 P.M., we ran out of gas. In those days there was not much traffic on Route 93. We were stranded.

Finally, a large truck and trailer stopped to give us a hand. The driver had a long chain, and he offered to pull us into Kingman. It was very cold and no other cars had gone by us, and I accepted. What a mistake! The driver attached a chain about thirty-foot long to our front bumper. We set off, and I sweated through twenty-five miles of nothing but curves. We had no power steering or power brakes, and as we went around the curves, the chain slackened, and sparks would fly up from the road. We would slow down, then jerk, slow down, then jerk. With no power brakes or power steering, I was tiring, and I couldn't get the truck driver's attention. After the best part of an hour, we finally got to Kingman. I was exhausted but very, very happy. My bumper was bent into a large "V" shape, but it had held. It was Christmas morning, 1962. Later that day, we got back safely to our rental home in Vegas. Although I intended just to "pass through Vegas, I ended up staying there for over forty-three years.

We lived in the rental home until I finished building our new house on Jerry Drive where I ran our fledgling business out of my home office for the first two years. In 1963 I was making more money than I ever had earned before.

My business did so well, that in late 1963, I teamed up with Leroy Cotter, and we bought Neptune Pools. With the acquisition of Neptune, we could begin building pools. Needing more help, and learning that Pat Shaughnessy was going through some rough times and needed work, I contacted him to see if he wanted to come to Vegas to help me out. Leaving his family in Phoenix for the time he would be working for me, he came to Vegas.

Bad Company

Things were going great. I ran Marine Tile, and Leroy built the new pools. However, the partnership didn't last long. Leroy started stealing from Neptune pool company, and I had to fire him.

I began to get suspicious when Leroy purchased two expensive two-way radios. Since we had no employees, I couldn't figure out why he thought we needed them. Next, I noticed unexplained charges and withdrawals in Neptune's bank statements. Large amounts of money had disappeared, and I had no idea where it went. My Neptune Pool business was gutted, and I was in deep trouble. Angry, I went to find Leroy.

When I did locate him, the conversation was short. I said, "I'm done with you, Leroy," and I fired him.

I had to get things straightened out. My reputation was on the line. I rushed to the bank to check my accounts. It was a disaster. Checks had bounced all over the place. Compounding the mess, without my permission, the bank had illegally covered the bounced Neptune Pool Company checks by raiding my personal account to cover the overdrafts. Even the funds from my personal account failed to cover all the outstanding checks, and I had to finish paying the rest from my Marine tile and coping business account. I was really angry. I didn't know at the time that it was against the law for the bank to raid my personal account to cover the overdrafts. I could have sued them, but being young and naive, I didn't know any better.

At the Same Time . . .

Although my business consumed a great deal of my effort and interest, I did not neglect church. Diane and I became active in the Red Rock Church in Las Vegas almost as soon as I arrived in town in 1962. In 1963, because of my background, the church made me building chairman for their new addition. As others learned about me, I was asked to help out in the building of two other churches in Las Vegas.

Over the years I spent at Red Rock, I felt restless about what I should be doing with the rest of my life. I even started thinking about the mission field. When my business became well established, I found I had the funds to travel. In hopes of settling the issue, I traveled to various mission fields in South America in an attempt to settle that matter in my own mind.

I had helped in the building program of three churches: Red Rock, West Oakey and First Southern

Baptist. Darryl Evanson was pastor at First Southern Baptist. His brother, Kenny, was a missionary in Uruguay, South America. Kenny was leaving the mission field and going to work in the United States translating the Bible.

In November, 1967, accompanied by Pastor Evanson, along with Kenny, his assistant, I flew to Montevideo, the capital of Uruguay. We planned to visit churches there, and Darryl and Kenny preached in many churches as we traveled north.

Touring South America, we traveled to Paraguay, Uruguay, Argentina, Chile, Bolivia, Brazil, Colombia, and ended up in Quito, Ecuador. The Voice of America radio station was based in Quito where Darryl and Kenny preached on the radio.

Darryl left for home on December fifteenth, but I stayed. I wanted to go into the jungle and stay at the halfway house where missionaries come out of the jungle for some R & R.

Elisabeth Elliot, the widow of Jim Elliot, one of the missionaries killed by the Auca natives in 1956, ran the retreat. I had a letter of introduction given to me by the man who ran the World Broadcasting Station, and Mrs. Elliot welcomed me and invited me to stay a few days. Her house was large with private rooms and a central dining area. The mission was an eight-hour bus ride from Quito. It was a beautiful trip through the jungle, and the road ended at the Elliot house. From that point there were no more roads. I spent a few days visiting with the missionaries who were there for R & R.

Traveling back, I spent that Christmas on the way home. I was sorry that Diane did not want to accompany me on that trip, or on any of my other trips.

Through those trips and contacts, I discovered my heart was not at peace with changing the direction my life by going on the mission field. Every time I traveled to visit another missionary station, I'm afraid my prayer went something like, "Lord, I'm willing to do whatever

You want me to do, but please don't call me to go on the mission field."

Returning home, I threw myself into my Marine Tile and Coping business.

I had started in business simply by setting tile and coping, but since there was no manufacturer of coping in Las Vegas, I had to have all my coping trucked in from Los Angeles. Since each piece of coping that I set around the perimeter of a pool was about twelve inches deep and eighteen inches long and weighed about forty pounds, shipping it in by the truckload was expensive. Some of the pools I worked on were in colder areas during winter months, and I had trouble finding tile that would survive cold temperatures without cracking. Cold temperatures demanded a special kind of tile, and there was no distributer that I knew of in Los Angeles for that special kind of tile. It was available from a distributer in Ohio, but to truck it in was a huge expense for my little company.

Expanding

All through 1963 I was still growing my business, and I needed to save on overhead. To solve the coping issue, I decided to manufacture my own.   I still had contacts in Phoenix, so I got in my truck, drove to Phoenix, and spoke to old man Jenson who owned "Jensen Patio and Brick Yard." I discovered Jensen had a spare set of fiberglass molds and a mixer that he was willing to sell.

"Take this, Danny," he said. "Pay me when you can."

I felt great. I went to see my friend, John Marshall at Sands Chevrolet and bought my first brand new one-ton truck, a 1962 Chevrolet flat-bed.

Driving back to Jensen's, I loaded the molds and mixer onto my new truck and headed back to Vegas. Just like that, I was now in the coping manufacturing and related pool products business. Although Jensen's molds were old and well-used, it was a start. My "Manufacturing plant" was the back yard of my first house. Eventually I bought better fiberglass molds and rented a building on a one-acre plot of land where I could make my product more efficiently.

I still had to figure out how to solve the problem of obtaining cold-weather tile at a reasonable cost. I learned that there was a Japanese manufacturer who produced frost-resistant tile. I decided my best move would be to go to Japan to see if I could develop a contact and find a supplier who would ship directly to me; but I wasn't yet able to leave the business to travel. The solution to the frost-resistant tile problem would have to wait.

I think of 1964 as a pivotal year because many major developments were crammed into twelve months

We had our fourth child, Matthew James, on October 1, 1964. My wife Diane and I were both RH negative. Three of our children had to have blood transfusions, out with the old blood and in with the new. Only Danny, our first, didn't need to have his blood replaced. The next major change was that we bought a new house on Jerry Drive.

Zell

Also, in 1964, my double cousin, Zell came to live with us for about a year. He had gone through some hard times, so we had taken him in. Zell was handy with tools. If it was broken, he could fix it. If it needed building, he could build it. As Zell started to get over his personal issues, I took him on as a helper. Eventually I put him in charge of manufacturing my copings, but that didn't work out quite as I had intended.

Without my permission, Zell decided to use my molds, equipment, and materials to create a little side business of his own. He made about four-hundred castings and sold them to a contact in Phoenix who had set up a business there to sell copings to local pool construction companies. The business in Phoenix failed, and Zell's customer was left holding four- hundred coping molds that he could not sell. At about forty pounds each, those concrete copings lying out in his customer's yard weighed close to eight tons. When I discovered what Zell had done, learned where the copings were, and what had happened with his client's business, I decided to capitalize on the situation. I offered to pay $1,000 for the lot if Zell's customer would transport them the copings to Vegas., He accepted my offer, and I was delighted. The thousand bucks for the four hundred molds was a drop in the bucket, even counting the cost of my materials to manufacture them, and I didn't have to make the molds myself. This was a great move, and it was the first really good thing that happened to me in Las Vegas.

Because I had to fire Leroy Cotter when I discovered he was stealing from the company, I put Zell in charge of running Neptune pools. It wasn't long before Zell told me that he was hearing around town that Leroy was looking for me, and that Leroy, "...wanted to beat the tar out of me."

I didn't like looking over my shoulder. At over six-feet tall, and weighing about 250 pounds, Leroy was a big man. I knew that sooner or later, we would have a run-in.

That encounter came one day when I was at a coping yard doing some business. Leroy and his brother Leonard pulled into the parking area out front. I could tell that trouble was coming. Taking off my glasses and my watch, I walked outside.

Leroy saw me, and he had hatred in his eyes. Jumping out of the truck, Leroy came at me like a wild bull. He took a swing at me, and I dodged away from the blow. As I dodged, I noticed that he closed his eyes when he threw a punch. I slipped my Chapstick into my right hand. He rushed at me, closing his eyes again. He couldn't see my blow coming, and I hit him on the chin and he went down. I pounced on him and picked up a piece of concrete, but decided not to hit him with it. Thinking the fight was over, I let him up. I could have knocked him cold, but I chose not to. Getting back up on his feet, Leroy still wanted to whip me so I told him, "All right, Let's go out behind the railroad cars and get it over with." He agreed, and we went out back to finish.

Again, he rushed me, and again he closed his eyes when he threw a punch. We were both tired and bleeding, but I landed another hard punch right on his chin, and he went down. By now I knew I could whip him so this time I didn't jump on him. Leroy got up slowly and stuck out his hand, "Danny," he said, "You're a better man than I thought." I hit him again and stuck out my hand. Leroy shook it. We never tangled again.

Frost-Free Tile

In 1964 I decided I could no longer put off that trip to Japan to obtain frost-free tile. The coldest freeze in more than fifty years had hit Las Vegas in January, 1963, and it had affected the tiles in all the pools in the city. The pools had ceramic tile above the water line, and when the freeze came, it popped the glaze on the pool tiles. Without the glaze protecting the tile, water wicked inside the base and expanded the tile until it broke.

At that time, I knew of only one place in the United States where I might buy tile, Romany Tile in Ohio, and trucking it in was very expensive. I anticipated doing a lot of pools in the coming months, and I needed a less-expensive source for frost-free tiles.

Early in 1964, I had decided I needed to follow up on a tip concerning a frost-free tile source in Japan, and after several months, I was finally ready to act. I decided to go to Japan..

A trip to Japan would be my first trip to a foreign country; obviously, I needed to get a passport. When I went to the passport office with my documentation, I discovered that although everyone had always called me, "Danny," the name on my birth-certificate was "Robert Henderson."

As I waited for my passport to arrive in the mail, I made travel arrangements. A friend in Red Rock Church was planning a trip to Tokyo to see his son stationed there while in the Air Force. When my friend learned I planned to go to Japan on business, he not only invited me along, but also he offered to put me up. I jumped at the chance, and I asked Diane if she wanted to go also. She told me, again, that I should go by myself.

A few weeks later my friend and I flew to Tokyo. When we got off the plane, his son picked us up and drove us to his house. My friend's son had his own car, and over the next couple of days, we spent some time sight-seeing. I climbed Mount Fuji and sampled some really great food. We toured Tokyo, and I thought the downtown section was the newest, most modern city I had ever seen. The streets were wide, the buildings were modern, and the trains were fast.

But having business to deal with, I found my way through Tokyo to the World-Wide Trade Show and searched for the manufacturer of the tile I needed. Although I found nothing there, I did learn that the tile I needed was made near Nagoya, a hundred-mile trip from Tokyo by bullet train. Reaching Nagoya, I transferred to a small local train and traveled to a village called Tajimi where many of the homes had small warehouses where the tile was made and where the raw material coming down from the nearby mountains was stored. I learned that in the process of manufacturing the tile, the major expense was the placing of the matting into the tile.. Trying to make a business contact so I could import their tile, I went from place to place, but I was unsuccessful.

Tajimi tiles are among the finest in the world

Disappointed, I returned to the Grand Hotel in Nagoya. Feeling I had made almost no progress, I settled into my room and started preparing to return to Tokyo when someone knocked on my door. I opened it to find an elderly Japanese man standing there. He bowed politely and said in perfect English, "I heard you were looking for tile."

"Yes," I answered.

"I am Mr. Yamasuta. I may have what you need. I am a tile distributer in Los Angeles.

I was stunned. I had traveled halfway around the world only to find that what I needed was to be had in Los Angeles.

The next morning Mr. Yamata took me back to Tajimi to introduce me to the people I needed to know. I was struck by both their generosity and their friendliness. I learned quickly to avoid admiring anything; for if I were to do so, I would immediately have it offered as a gift, and it would be an insult for me to refuse. Mr. Yamata guided me through Tajimi's many little factories producing a variety of patterns of mosaic tile. He helped me make connections and arrangements that led to my making a deal to purchase tile from the largest factory in the village. That business arrangement in Tajimi lasted for the next forty years. Pleased that I had solved my problem of finding a source of frost-resistant tiles, I returned home and went back to growing my business and back to Diane. She had missed

a good time. I hoped she would come with me on my

next trip.

Happier times. Diana and I, 1965

Stolen Molds

My business flourished. I had most of the tile coping business in town, but it wasn't without its challenges. One morning I went to my coping manufacturing yard to discover that all my fiberglass coping molds had been stolen. I was angry. It was the middle of the summer, my busiest time.

A friend of mine, a local tile-setter, gave me a lead as to who stole my molds. I called my lawyer, George Crommer, Sr. and explained to him what had happened, that Gordon Brown, a terrazzo contractor, knew who had stolen my molds. George told me to get some of my employees, find Gordon and take him out to the desert and get the name of the thief from him.

The next morning we found Brownie at Bonanza Tile. I stomped into Bonanza Tile's office and confronted him. We ended up in a fist fight in the parking lot. I knocked him out, dragged him to my pickup, and my employees and I dumped him in the back. As Brownie started to regain consciousness, we heard the police sirens. Brownie was scared, and he told us that Bill Small had stolen the molds. He jumped off the truck; my men piled in the bed of my pickup, and I took off.

I called George to tell him what had happened, and he told me to go to the police station and accuse Brownie of starting a fight with me. He said if I did this, they wouldn't put me in jail, and it would turn into a civil case. That's exactly what I did, and I heard no more about the incident.

Determined to get my molds back, I phoned Information and found Bill Small's address in Tucson, Arizona. That evening, I got my brother-in-law, Bob Leedom, and Leroy Fisher, an employee of mine, and we took off for Tucson in my 1962 Chevy Impala. It was the first car I owned with air-conditioning, and even driving through the hot night, we really appreciated the way the air conditioner kept us cool. Rolling into Tucson about

6:00 A.M. on a Sunday morning, we found Bill's home, a small block house with no garage. There was no place there to store my molds.

I felt dumb for coming all this way and not being able to find the molds. Not wanting to waste our trip, we decided to take the short drive to Mexico and spend the day there instead. As we pulled out on Blackstone Boulevard, I asked God to help us. In fact, I prayed the Lord would take the steering wheel and lead us to the molds. I had about a grain of mustard seed sized faith in that prayer. As we continued down Blackstone Boulevard, we passed a pool company building with a "Thunderbird Pools" sign on front. Figuring I had nothing to lose, I pulled into the driveway and drove around back where I saw a number of storage units. We looked around as we drove slowly past the units. I was just about to leave when I turned and noticed the word, "Smalls" written in pencil.   I got out of the car to looked inside, and I couldn't believe what I saw. Yes, oh, yes, there were my molds.

By now, it was about 7:00 A.M., and the rental yards had just opened where we could rent a trailer. As quickly as we could, we rented the largest trailer my car could haul and went back to "Thunderbird Pools," broke the lock off the storage unit, and loaded up the molds. As we drove out, the trailer hitch on my soft-sprung Impala was about six inches off the ground. We were very nervous as we headed back to Vegas at about 40 miles per hour. It took a long time to get home, but it was a happy drive. I had my molds; we had our air-conditioning, and we were back in business.

Secrets

Disclosure

It was 1971, and my life changed drastically.

Walter Arnold and his family, Nancy, Chuck and Timmy, plus my family, Diana, Danny, Lois, Debbie and Matt, rented a motorhome, and we all took a trip back east. We visited New York and Washington, D.C. Then we traveled down the rest of the east coast to Florida. From Florida we went west all across the south. All seemed to be going well, but by the time we got to Oklahoma, I sensed a change.

The mood in the motor home seemed to have developed some kind of tension. I couldn't figure out what had changed. I knew something was going on; I had no idea what it was, and I didn't like it.

By the time we got back to Las Vegas, about midnight, I became a bit upset because my new 1972 Cadillac was missing from the driveway where I had parked it . When we left for our trip. Diane's brother, Bobby was to stay at our house while we were gone, and he wasn't supposed to be driving it.

When we all went inside the house, I looked at Walter and said, "Why would he upset me by taking my car?"

Walter looked back at me with a serious expression on his face. "You've got bigger problems than that, Danny," he said, "Let's go upstairs."

Immediately I thought that something was wrong with Diane. Someplace in Oklahoma, during one of our stops, Diane had made a call from a pay phone. I didn't think too much of it at the time, for she had called her friend, Sally, several times during our trip; but there was something different this time. As I had watched her on the phone, her face had turned white, and she looked as

I had never seen her before. I didn't know whom she was talking to, and my mind jumped to the worst thing I could think of. Did she have cancer? I had the same kinds of scary thoughts I had the night the mood among all the other people in the RV had changed in Oklahoma.

Leaving the women downstairs, Walter and I went up to my bedroom.

"Sit down, Ike," he said. He always called me "Ike."

Then he gave me the bad news. "Your wife and Larry have been having an affair."

"What?" I was stunned.   My wife and Larry Lewis? The youth and choir director at our church? An affair? And for five years?

Walter went on to tell me that the first time they had gotten caught was three years into the affair. Finally, now five years into the affair, when we were in Washington D.C., on one of her frequent telephone calls, Sally told Diane that she and Larry had been seen, and that the matter had been brought before the Deacons. Now I understood why Diane had been upset. At last, everything had spilled out into the open. Not once in the whole five years that she was having the affair with Larry did I ever suspect it. Even though the whole church seemed to have known about it, no one had ever breathed a word to me. I felt like a fool, and I was angry.

Walter had little else he could say, and we sat in awkward silence. I thanked him. We stood, shook hands, and he went slowly down the stairs and left.

I sat on the bed for a moment to think. I didn't want Larry and Diane to get together to fabricate some kind of self-excusing story; so even though it was close to one in the morning, I decided Larry was going to get a visitor tonight, and it would not be a social call.

Confrontation

I drove over to Larry's house to confront him. I knocked on the door, and Larry let me in. He and his wife, Beverly, had been sitting up waiting for me so I figured Diane had called to tell them I was on my way over. When I sat down and confronted Larry about why he had entered into an affair with my wife, all he said that it was ". . .only a brief encounter," and that "The Devil made me do it." Then he told me that the affair was over.

All the while, as I spoke, Beverly just sat and stared.

I looked at Larry and said, "Stay away from my wife. If you don't, there will be bad consequences." I left, got in my car, and drove home. By then, it was about two o'clock in the morning.

When I got home, Diana was still up. When I told her what Larry had said, she was very upset. I went upstairs to bed, but I didn't sleep much the rest of that night.

The next several weeks were gloomy ones. Then, one day I listened in while Diane was on the phone and discovered that she and Larry were still seeing each other. I'd had enough.

Larry played tennis at the Desert Inn. I put my Colt .45 single-action six-shot revolver under my front seat. I planned to drive over to the Desert Inn and have another "little talk" with him. When I got to the Desert Inn, I pulled the gun out from under the seat and slipped a cartridge into just one of the six chambers of the revolver. I planned to play some Russian roulette with Larry. When I saw him, I would walk up to him, point the gun at his head, and pull the trigger. He would have a one-in-six chance to go on living. If the gun hit an empty chamber, I would open the pistol, pitch him the bullet and tell him if there was a second time with my wife, the gun would have six shells in it.

However, Larry wasn't playing tennis that morning. I got back in my car and drove home.

Graham's Advice

A couple of weeks later, Diana told me she wanted to go San Francisco to see my doctor friend, Graham Reedy, and get some marriage counseling. After she left to see Graham, Beverly, Larry's wife, called and told me Larry was in Castro Valley, California at a church revival. She was thoroughly disgusted with Larry and wanted me to go after him..

Chance encounter with Diane? Not likely. Castro Valley was in San Leandro, just across the bay from San Francisco. More lies.

Determined that I wouldn't miss him a second time, I got my buck knife and slipped it into my overnight bag. I planned to castrate Larry. That would end the affair once and for all. I drove to the airport, parked my car in the long-term lot, bought my ticket, and boarded a plane to San Francisco.

When I landed in San Francisco, I called Graham Reedy. He was a Doctor now, and I had known him since we were students at Christian High. When I told him what I had planned, he urged me to wait at the airport, and he would pick me up. When Graham picked me up, I could see he had a high level of concern.

Graham drove me back to his house and sat me down over a cup of coffee

"Danny," he said. "I don't know what I'd do if I was in your shoes. Nobody can really say that.

"However, that's bygones, and you've got four kids. Think about them and their Mom. Do you really want to do this thing?   Then you're going to go to trial and go to jail. Are you going to keep stirring this horrible thing up?

"Don't do it, Danny. Don't do it. You've got better sense than that."

Graham looked at me. I could see his concern in his face.

"Stay with me a week or two," he said, "You know, until you get better control of yourself."

I trusted Graham. Over all the years since Christian High, we had kept in contact. He was the team physician for the Raiders, and I had often gone to football games with him.   Graham had given me a lot to think about, and I considered the fallout of what I had planned to do. I spent several days with him and then flew back to Vegas.

The Sunday after I got back was the last time I attended to Red Rock Church. Larry led the music, his wife, Beverly, was in the choir. When Larry started to lead in prayer, I couldn't stand the hypocrisy. Miserable, I got up, left the service to walk out to the front of the church and to stand in the breezeway. With my family still in church, I couldn't yet leave.

As I brooded about what I had learned about Larry in the last few months, I felt as if someone had hit me in the belly with a baseball bat. Here, Larry was up front, leading singing in my church. Everyone in the church— except me—had known that he was still having an affair with my wife, that this affair was not his first but simply another in a series of affairs. I had heard Larry had been involved with other women at various other churches. Each time he was discovered, he was kicked out of one church after another.

I left the breezeway and sat outside in my car waiting for the service to end. I saw Beverly come out. She must have felt the same way I did and had left the choir loft to come outside.

Beverly was a beautiful, sweet person, and she was pretty – prettier than my wife. With such a beautiful wife, I could never figure out why Larry was fooling around with my Diane.

We talked a little while. Beverly was angry and wanted revenge. She asked me to have sex with her to get even with Diana and Larry. She did have her revenge with an old boyfriend. That was the last time I saw Beverly.

I had seen, heard, and experienced enough. Emotionally and spiritually I was devastated. It was over a year later before I walked through another church door.

Sometime later I learned more about how Larry and Diane had been discovered the first time. Three years earlier, and Glen Maxie, a plumber and a deacon at our church, had seen them at a hotel and reported this to Pastor Loving. Having been found out, Diane and Larry told the Pastor that the romance was over. No one ever told me about that episode at that time.

The romance wasn't over. Two years later, a friend of mine, also a member of Red Rock Church, flew a helicopter for the Police Department. One day, while he was flying, he got a call about a stolen 1972 Cadillac. He spotted the vehicle and dropped a little closer to check license plates. It wasn't the stolen car. It was registered to me. Next to my car, he spotted Larry's Volkswagen. This time their romance was reported to the deacons for a second time, and Larry was asked to resign.

I saw Larry one last time. I don't remember the occasion, but we met at a "Mom and Pop" hamburger place over near my house. I told him how I missed him with the gun and later with the knife. He started to cry and told me how lucky I was to get Diana and the Oscar pool cleaner I had developed. He was pitiful, and I gave him no mercy. In my opinion, he was lucky to be alive and whole, and so was I. Beverly divorced him a couple of months later. The last I heard of Larry is that he went to Thailand.

Finally, I did figure out why Larry was after my wife when he had such a beautiful wife of his own. It was money. Larry made only a modest salary as a Choir director and youth leader in our church. During their affair, Diane told him that we had been offered $750,000 for our business. Larry must have figured that Diane would get a windfall in a divorce and then he could get together with her.

Loneliness

About three months after I had learned of Diana's affair with Larry, her brother, Bobby, pulled up in front of our hous in a large U-Haul truck. They loaded her things, and Diana with three of my children left Vegas for Phoenix. I sat in the empty lot next door and wept. I could not believe my three children were gone. Only Danny, my oldest son, had stayed with me. Three months later, however, nine-year-old Matt, my youngest son, came back to live with me.

During this time I learned that Diana's mother, Juanita, was working as a waitress. I had my hands full with taking care of the home, raising the boys, and running the business. I needed help, and I offered Diana's mother a job as a live-in housekeeper, helper with the boys, and as a helper with the office-work in the business. She accepted my offer. I paid her $100 per week plus room and board. Juanita loved me and the boys, and she stayed with us for a little more than a year. After leaving me, she moved back to Iowa and died a short time later.

During that year, I called and wrote letters to Diana trying to persuade her to come back to Vegas. She did return, but it was only for one of the kids' parties. As we had to go someplace in my car, I had a chance to talk with her.

"Diana," I said, "We've got four kids. Are you sure you're done with me?"

"I'm sure," she said.

We divorced, and I moved on. Diane, however, kept showing her bitterness toward me in various ways over the next thirty years by spreading lies about me, limiting my contact with the children, and making things as inconvenient as possible in family gatherings. The kids were caught in the middle. Finally, one day our daughter, Lois, had had enough. She glared at Diane and said, "Mom, Dad's here. Deal with it."

Diane did everything she could to try to get the kids to leave me and come to live with her, but every time they tried living with her, they came right back to my house.

Oscar

Big Bucks

When I came to Vegas in 1962, I made friends with a man named Marty Ross. Now, in 1970, I decided to invite him on as a partner in my new endeavor. We named the business, "Vegas Outdoor Products."   We had learned of a prototype of an automatic pool cleaner. Moore, the man who developed it was the same person who invented the coin-operated car wash. We decided to invest and paid him $5,000 for the rights to manufacture it under our own name.

To deal with the complicated details of setting up our business and new invention, Marty and I went to Washington, D.C. where we hired an attorney.   He helped us apply for patents for our pool cleaner in South Africa, Australia, England, France, Spain, Germany and the United States. By the end of 1971 we ended up with patents in these seven countries. At the same time we were building our nine injection molds. The patents, the molding tools, and the brochure cost about $150,000. By early 1972 the largest mold was almost finished, and we owed $50,000. I had been working very hard to maintain my home, my pool business and to make enough to pay for the cleaner molds. Marty and I owed $25,000 each. Marty had his half, but I didn't have my half. However, on my birthday December 31, 1971, Diana gave me a $20,000 cashier's check. It was the best birthday present I ever got.

I'm pretty sure Diana had been saving money with the intention of leaving me, but she got greedy and put it off. She knew we had been offered $750,000 for Vegas Outdoor Products.

In November, 1972 the National Swimming Pool Institute held its yearly convention in Las Vegas. We had made a deal to build a small swimming pool at the convention site and to display our new pool cleaner. The brochures and tooling were done, and when the pool show opened, we were ready.

The cleaner we developed was the second automatic cleaner ever invented. We named it "Oscar."

When the doors opened and the convention began, Oscar was a great success. We took orders for about three thousand cleaners at that show. We were really on our way. The only other cleaner, the Arneson Pool Sweep, patent #004, sold at a distributor price of $230 each. Our cleaner sold to distributors that bought 500 at a time for $60 each. Right off, at the convention, we sold 3,000 cleaners: 500 in Florida, 500 in Los Angeles, 500 in England, and 500 to Gary Creighton at Tropicana Pool in Florida. We took orders for additional 1,000 Oscars here in the U.S.

Oscar Pool Cleaner in action

Murphy's Law

Murphy's Law states, "Whatever can go wrong will go wrong."

Marty and I remained partners for four years, but the stresses of the business caused friction between us and, by 1975, we were not getting along. Marty offered either to buy me out, or I could buy him out. Certain that "Oscar" would continue to grow in value, I chose the latter.

I knew some people in the Channel Islands, and I contacted them and offered to grant them exclusive rights to distribute Oscar in Europe. As an incentive, I added a set of coping molds that were made in Florida. They gave $130,000 for the deal.

Then in 1976 the energy crunch hit the country. Having many orders for Oscar, I suddenly faced difficulty in filling them because of a sudden shortage of ABS, PVC, and Lexon, all materials we used to produce the cleaners.

I finally found a material made by General Electric called "Buterick," a material used in building motor homes. Because of the recession, motor home sales were down, and plenty of the material we needed was available. G.E. guaranteed their material would work for our pool cleaner.

I put in an order for 5,000 cleaners. When the different parts started to arrive, I had made a deal with the rehabilitation center in Vegas to assemble and box our cleaners.

About this time I got a letter from Mutual Construction in Sydney, Australia. Al Hooper, CEO of Mutual Pools, told me it cost $20 tax on each Oscar, and he wanted a licensing agreement to produce the Oscar in Australia. It sounded great to me, and I flew to Sydney; but when I arrived they told me the factory had burned down.   I thought they meant the factory in Melbourne where I was supposed to go to help in the design of the new pool cleaner. I soon found out, however, rather than the Melbourne factory, it was the rehabilitation warehouse in Las Vegas that had burned down.

Producing injection molds for "Oscar"

I made the deal with Mutual Pools in Australia and flew back to Las Vegas to straighten out the problems caused by the fire at the rehabilitation center. Most of our products had been destroyed so I ordered 5,000 more cleaners. As they arrived, I decided to assemble them at my own warehouse. A few months later we began getting complaints about the Oscar blowing out its manifold. We had a very large problem.

As we struggled to solve the Oscar problem, I got a shock from the Ninth Circuit Court in San Francisco. Andrew Panzini was suing me for patent infringement.

Panzini had invented the first automatic swimming pool cleaner, the "Pool Sweep." He then sold the "Pool Sweep" to Arneson with the stipulation that Panzini would retain the patent rights. Because our Oscar sold so well and had begun to cut into Arneson's sales of his Pool Sweep, Panzini sued me for patent infringement. Arneson sold the Pool Sweep to Castle & Cook Corp who owned Dole Pineapple and many more companies in America.

I called my patent attorney, and he came from Washington, D.C. to San Francisco. Panzini had to defend the 044 patent he had sold to Arneson. When the trial was over, I lost the patent infringement case. I met with Castle & Cook attorneys and made a licensing agreement. I was to pay a $10 royalty with no minimums. In addition, I had to pay their lawyer, my lawyer and the court costs. To settle the accounts, I sold about $70,000 worth of Oscars. When everything was settled, I was out of debt and out of money. I sold Vegas Outdoor Products to my son-in-law for $50,000.

Earlier that year I had sold Marine Tile and Coping to my oldest son, Danny, for $100,000.

Chris

Second Family

With the emotional trauma over Diane, the complications with the patents, and the kids having grown, I found I didn't take the same pleasure in my work anymore. I started to feel like a boat cut loose from its moorings and set adrift.

I had been single for over a year, and although my kids all lived with me, my personal life was in a shambles. That whole episode with Larry, Diane, and the embarrassment of being made of fool of, had left a bitter taste in my mouth about Church things, and I had given up attending.

I felt a little helpless. I had a bunch of kids to raise, and I had no one to help me. I needed something or someone to hold onto and to gain some emotional stability.

One day, while I was visiting Walter and Nancy Arnold, we went to a ball game where I met Chris Kidd. I had known her in high school but hadn't seen her since I graduated almost twenty years before. We had a short three-month courtship, and because we both needed help in raising our children, as a matter of practicality, in the summer of 1974, we decided to marry and add Chris's three children, Cassie, Travis and Bubba, to my four.

I had not yet met her three children, and Chris had not yet met my four kids; but when we all came together, we found that Chris was good with my kids and I with hers. All the kids went together at Clark High School. Before they all graduated, I had built a pool for

Mr. Johnson, the principal, and Lanny Lund, a teacher there at Clark.

Combined family: Chris Kidd, Cassie, Lois, and Debbie

With Chris and her children, I found a normalcy in my life that had been missing for a long time. I felt comfortable in becoming the head of the family, and I reconnected with the church – not Red Rock, but our mission Church, West Ockey. My son, Danny, played the piano, and all the kids sang in the choir. We stayed as members of the West Ockey Church for ten years.

As a family, we also enjoyed many outings together in fishing, water-skiing and snow-skiing as well as hunting. I also took the boys to the Super Bowl. Life was full, and sometimes a little frantic, but at last we got all the kids graduated, including Scott, my sister's boy, who had stayed with us during his Senior year.

By the time the kids were gone, Chris and I had been married for eleven years. I didn't know if I was tired, restless, or just needed a change. Chris and I had married more out of a recognition of practicality than that of passion. I asked her for a divorce, and she agreed. There were no hard feelings.

I went to my lawyer and gave Chris our five-bedroom house on which we owed about $10,000. So she would have money to pay off the mortgage, I added $20,000 in cash and I also gave her the car. I took on all our debts. I was adrift again.

Travel

Empty Heart

I was single again, and I loved it. Freed from restraints of family, business, and even of church, and with no one to answer to or to hold me accountable, I sowed my wild oats - drugs, alcohol and women. I had no intention to marry again – ever..

I bought a duplex. My son Matt bought the other half. The rest of my kids were already married.

I still owned Danny Henderson Enterprises, Kool Deck and Concrete-Desert Gem Pools.

Matt and I built spas in our back yards. My daughter, Lois, and her husband, Kirby, got a divorce; and Lois, with her three children, moved in with Matt.

With no particular business responsibilities to keep me at home, I remembered how much I had enjoyed travelling. That first trip to Japan had always brought pleasant memories, and so I decided to travel again and to explore new places.

My passports with stamps from over sixty countries.

Anything I have ever done, I have done with enthusiasm and energy – well, except for the going to college time. Between 1964 and 2001, I toured sixty countries all over the world. I travelled all through countries in South America, eastern Europe, western

Europe, England, Scotland, Ireland, Egypt, Israel, Turkey, Australia, Canada, Mexico, Japan, Panama, Belize, Guatemala and many Caribbean islands. In the States I took in Alaska and Hawaii. Matt sometimes accompanied me on some of these trips. I enjoyed having him with me in Belize and on my Amazon River trip, as well as on excursions closer to home when we went to Copper Canyon.

Belize

In September, 1988, Matt and I went to Belize to visit his friend, Kenny. From Belize, we took a small plane to Ambergris Key, a small island in the Caribbean which has the second largest barrier reef in the world. We landed at San Pedro Airport and went to the northern end of the island to the Playa del Sol Resort where we stayed in a cabin about fifty yards from the water. The reef was about one-hundred yards from shore. We swam to the reef where the water was about four feet deep. As we swam we were surrounded by hundreds of all kinds of fish. I decided to dive down and grab a large leaf of seaweed, but I let go quickly when I discovered I had grabbed the tail of a large shark which headed straight for Matt but then turned and headed out to sea.

The next day we went fishing and caught all the fish we wanted. That evening we had a big fish dinner at the El Zifiro restaurant. At that time Belize was celebrating its independence from England, and it was like the fourth of July. Many British sailors, along with the locals were celebrating Belize's independence from British rule. They crowded every restaurant and bar and strode up and down the unpaved streets singing and shouting.

We found one bar that was decorated like an old-fashioned sailing ship. A brass ship's bell hung prominently near the entrance, and as we entered, everyone shouted, "Ring the bell! Ring the bell!" I figured, "Why not?" I gave a smart yank on the lanyard hanging from the clapper and a loud – and expensive – CLANG rang through the room. Everyone shouted and whooped. Ringing that bell meant I had to buy everyone drinks!

Another place we visited faced the small harbor. A circle of poles formed a sort of pen for sharks when the tide surged in. The boozy sailors amused themselves by throwing each other into the shark pen. We had a lot of fun that night.

The next day as we ate at a local restaurant, CNN reported that hurricane "Hugo" was coming straight at us, and the island people began boarding up their windows. Others, I guess they were local fishermen, rolled their boats out of the water on big logs.

CNN had warned of a fifteen-foot tide surge. The island we were on was about five hundred yards wide and a mile long, and the greatest concern of the people was that the highest point in Ambergris Key was only sixteen feet above sea level. In addition, there were few concrete or stone houses on the island. Matt and I found a new two-story concrete house under construction. The upstairs was still unfinished. We found some rope and tied it to a concrete pillar. We planned to tie ourselves to the pillar when the water hit the island. With the storm still a couple of hours away, we walked back to our cabin. Tired from all the activity of the day, we stretched out on our beds and promptly fell asleep only to wake up to the crash of a large bird smashing into our window. We got up and went outside. The water was right at our door. The generator on the island was turned off at midnight, and it was inky, black dark.

Matt was naked as he walked out on the beach into about two feet of water. Then, suddenly the lights flashed on. People from surrounding cabins had also come outside in the blackout, and when the lights flooded the area, there was Matt without a stich of clothes on. All the people yelled and cheered and clapped their hands as Matt ran back to our cabin.

Fortunately, hurricane Hugo missed us and turned North toward the Yucatan peninsula where it killed 6,000 people.

The next day we were ready to leave; and a small plane took us back to Belize, where we boarded a flight back to the States and home. As we flew northward, through the plane's window, we could see the storm clouds of the hurricane. Lightning flashed from cloud to cloud like flashes from heavy artillery in a great war. The storm hit Houston, Texas, where it did a lot more damage.

Mexico

Our next trip, in 1990, was to Copper Canyon, Mexico. We flew to Los Mochis, Mexico where we boarded a small train, the "Ferrocarril Barrancas del Cobre," which took us through Copper Canyon to Chihuahua. Copper Canyon is not a single canyon but rather a series of massive canyons in the Sierra Madre Mountain range. Copper Canyon gets its name from the copper-green hues on the walls of the canyons in the area. On that ride we crossed the Continental Divide four times, went through more than eighty tunnels, and crossed over forty bridges through some of the most rugged country I have ever seen. That evening we got off the train and spent the night at the Hotel Divisadero Barrancas near the railroad tracks The next morning we were on our way again.

Our next stop was an old Spanish mission, Barranca del Cobre. We had not seen any cars or trucks, in fact there were no roads at all.

Roads range from the primitive to none.

It had started to rain during the day, and it gradually turned into a downpour which caused a landslide that had washed out the train tracks. We found ourselves stranded at the Sixteenth Century Spanish mission, Barranca del Cobre. We stayed in the Hotel Divisadero Barrancas near the railroad tracks. The hotel had no phones or electric lights, and all we had for heat and light were wood-burning stoves and Coleman lanterns.

We enjoyed talking to the other passengers, and although they were from all over the world, many spoke English. When language failed, smiles, gestures and body language came to our rescue, and we made ourselves understood. At that time the United States had just invaded Kuwait. Needless to say, there were a lot of different views.

The next day was New Year's Eve, my birthday. A train from Chihuahua arrived to pick us up, and the other tourists got on board. Matt and I decided to stay behind. Because it was New Year's Eve, we knew we couldn't fly out, and there would be no place to stay in

Chihuahua. There, at the hotel, we were warm and comfortable; and we had new-found friends. Waving farewell to the other travelers, we watched the train growl and squeal off toward Chihuahua.

The two guys who worked at the mission had befriended us, and that evening they asked Matt and me if we wanted to go with them to a wedding reception about fifteen miles away where the Governor's daughter was getting married. Always ready for something new, of course, we agreed. We all piled into their old station wagon. Matt sat in the front next to the driver while I sat in the back next to the other worker, and the four of us were on our way. The workers had brought along two bottles of tequila, and we drove and drank and sang as we bounced along that fifteen miles to the reception. Thank God, Matt just faked drinking as we went along, and he saved us from disaster several times.

About sunset, we topped a hill and descended toward the little town. As we came closer, I saw a bride in a white dress dancing along with thousands of Mexicans in white cowboy hats. The white hats stretched out in front of us like a sea of white foam.

I don't remember much after that. I'm not a drinker, and the tequila I had swallowed must have gotten to me. I found myself joining in the dancing and merry-making. I must have been having a little too much fun because someone hit me so hard it knocked my glasses off. That's when I decided it was time to go.

By then it was about two or three o'clock in the morning, and Matt was ready to leave also. He searched through the crowd of dancing Mexicans trying to find the guys from the mission, but he had no luck. In addition, he found no one who could speak English. Finally, we found a guy who was willing to take us back to the hotel, but it would cost us fifty dollars. That wedding reception was the biggest party I have ever seen. There must have been five thousand people there.

The next morning, Matt, and I, fighting my tequila headache, found some kids who rented us their horses for the day. As we rode out of town, we heard everyone laughing at us; for they had recognized the two crazy Americans who had made fools of themselves at the reception. The whole town must have been there, but the only person we recognized was our fifty-dollar chauffer who had bounced us back over that fifteen-mile stretch of dirt road in the wee hours of the morning,

We rode the horses out to the nearby river and saw that the rain the night before had raised the water level so high that the town was in danger of flooding. Riding further upstream we came to a spectacular waterfall.

As we rode back through the little town, the people still pointed and laughed at us as we passed. A little later that day the railroad track was cleared, and we were on our way back to Los Mochis, and then home.

The Amazon

Another trip, in 1989, was a cruise down the Amazon River. Ever since the trip I had taken years before to Ecuador to visit the missionaries, I wanted to go down the Amazon, and this time I didn't go alone. My sister, Imogene, wanted to go with us, and Matt asked if we could take his cousin, Scott. Matt said it was Scott's birthday, and he thought it would be a lot of fun with him along. A couple weeks later we were on our way.

When we got to Iquitos, Peru, it was raining harder than we had ever seen before. We went to eat dinner, and though the food was new to us, we thoroughly enjoyed it. I asked what we were eating, They told us, "Monkey." That was the last time on that trip I asked that question.

The next morning we boarded our houseboat which carried about fifteen people, counting the captain and crew. My sister and I stayed in one cabin, and Scott and Matt occupied another.

The Amazon houseboat that carried our party.

At that time we didn't know the Amazon was one of the most dangerous rivers in the world. The river is ninety feet deep, and at its mouth, it's maybe twenty miles wide. There are enough fish in the river to feed half the people in the world.

The first afternoon of the trip, we stopped at a little native village. To see the little children, with their distended stomachs looking as if they had swallowed a watermelon, made me sad. The natives drink the river water without boiling it, and they all had parasites in their bodies.

Native village along the Amazon

When we went ashore to visit the little village, it didn't take long before we were trading with the natives. Scott had some little cars, and the children loved them. I had a Bic lighter. My sister had lipstick and a little mirror. Matt had some hard candy. We all did some trading. Carrying our treasures of blowguns, arrows, native artwork, and other trinkets, we returned to our boat.

As we cruised down the river, the captain told us to watch up ahead and we would see some pink dolphins. Yes, pink. Sure enough, as we came to a tributary we saw them. There were maybe fifty of the pink dolphins, jumping and diving all over the river. Our guide for our trip told us the dolphins were sacred to the natives.

The next day we visited another native village. Only seven of us went on the hike with our guide. Scott had decided to venture ahead, and he disappeared out of sight of our little group. Suddenly, I looked up to see him running back down the trail toward us. He was out of breath and excited. He said, "The people in the village ahead are all naked!"

Scott shot the dart and hit the post

When the rest of us arrived at the village, the little chief welcomed us with a demonstration of how to use a blowgun. He asked if anyone of our group wanted to try it. The natives had placed a post stuck in the ground as a target about twenty yards away. Matt tried first, and the dart just sort of dropped out the end of the blowgun. The natives roared with laughter. My attempt was worse, and the natives were even more amused.

Then Scott took the blowgun, shot the dart and hit the post. Everybody whooped and hollered, and the village chief made Scott acting chief. We did a little more trading, and then then headed back aboard the boat to continue our trip down the river.

The captain told us the greatest danger on the river was the giant trees floating half submerged in the water, and another hazard was the piranha. One day, when our boat stopped at a little village to deliver some goods, a few of us started fishing. We all had only a stick with a short fishing line and a hook at the end. All we had to do was put on some bait, drop the hook in the river, and bingo, we had a piranha.

Bingo! I had a piranha!

Piranhas have big heads and razor-sharp teeth. They are not very large, seldom longer than ten inches, but they are ferocious. A school of piranhas can strip a cow in less than one minute. Their teeth are so sharp that the South-American natives use them to make tools and weapons.

Even after being caught, a piranha can still be dangerous enough to take off flesh or a toe from a careless fisherman. Unaware of the danger, we would catch the fish and drop them on the floor to flop around and return to our fishing. Behind us, as we fished, the Captain's fourteen-year-old son walked by while a live piranhas still jumped around on the deck. The boy wasn't paying attention, and one of the piranhas grabbed fastened itself to his bare foot and bit out a chunk. After that we all were a little more careful when we fished.

The Captain's son before the piranha bit his foot

The next night we got to go caiman hunting. A caiman looks a lot like an alligator, but has a much more evil appearance. While the alligator has a broad, rounded snout and mostly covered teeth, the caiman has a long, narrow snout with many dagger-like teeth showing. They have slanted, yellow eyes. The natives catch them for their edible tails.

That evening, Scott, Matt, the guide, the pole man, and I got into a long dugout canoe and took off on the caiman hunt. We had a flashlight, and as we crept along the shore, we aimed the light along the water's edge.

Since the caiman hunts by lying with his mouth open waiting for his dinner to pass close by, we were able to spot it when its two orange eyes reflected back in the beam of our flashlight. Inching our way through the weeds near the bank, we headed for the orange eyes. Our pole man nudged us closer and closer. Our guide leaned over the front of our canoe with a flashlight in his mouth and a rope loop in his hand. Just as he lunged for the catch, Scott tried to move us a little closer. That was a mistake. Our guide missed with rope and almost fell into the river. We all were disappointed, especially Scott. When we got back to the boat, guess what we had for dinner. Yes, caiman. Another villager had delivered a caiman tail before we had gotten back.

The next day, as we cruised on down the river, along the bank we saw small huts built on stilts to sit about eight feet above the waterline. Our guide told us the houses were raised on stilts because, during the wet season, the river often would rise almost as high as the raised huts. We ended our river trip somewhere in Brazil.

Peru

Scott and I in Peru

Leaving the riverboat, we flew back to Lima, Peru, and caught a train to Machu Picchu. That train ride was one of the most beautiful scenic trips I have ever taken. As we went deeper and deeper into the jungle we passed giant mountains and rivers. We saw little villages where the people came out to wave to us as we passed by.

When we got to the end of the tracks, there were buses waiting for us. We loaded into the buses, and up, up, up we went, switchback after switchback until we finally arrived at the top of the world and Machu Picchu. Located in a saddle between two towering mountains, Machu Picchu is almost 8,000 feet high.

Machu Picchu

Machu Picchu, built out of large, carefully shaped stones, was not discovered until the early twentieth century. The beautiful stonework forming the buildings was set without mortar, and the stones were fit together so skillfully that where they met one against another, one can hardly put a knife between them.. How the Incas dragged those large stones up the steep mountain is still a mystery.

We spent most of the day exploring the three main rooms with their walls of polished stone, and we wandered among the out-buildings which were in the process of restoration. Tired at the end of the day, we returned to our buses and rode back down the switchbacks to our hotel.

The next day we headed next to Cuzco, Peru. At over 11,000 feet, the high altitude made it difficult for planes to take off. We spent a couple days visiting the town, and then we flew back to Lima. Instead of going straight home, we decided to take a side trip to Nassau

The Caribbean

After landing at Lindin Pindling International Airport in Nassau, we registered at the Holiday Inn Hotel. Wanting to see the sights, we rented a limousine to tour the island. That evening, after dinner, Scott and Matt went for a walk on the beach. When they got back to the hotel, they shared their adventure with us.

They really had gone to the beach looking for some marijuana, and they asked one of the locals where they could get some. He told them to wait, and he would be right back.

He returned soon with an ounce of marijuana in a brown paper sack and demanded a hundred dollars. Fearing they were in danger of someone interrupting their pot deal, they gave the guy his money and high-tailed it back to our room. When they opened the brown paper sack, Instead of marijuana, the sack was filled with crunched-up palm leaves. They had been ripped off. When the boys told me what had happened, I laughed until I almost cried. We all went to bed with no smoke.

The next morning we flew back to Miami. Still not ready to go home, we rented a car and drove to Key West, where, the boys finally thought they got their ounce of pot. Saving it until later, we spent the time shopping, eating conch soup and sightseeing.

The next day, as we were getting ready to leave, we discovered our pot was missing. We searched high and low but never found it. We thought we had been ripped off again.

The morning after we returned home, Scott was trying to get his steel-toed boots on, but he had trouble getting one of his feet inside the boot. When he reached inside his boot, there was the ounce of weed. When Scott told us, we knew we had dodged a bullet.

We had gone through the metal detector many times with Scott's steel-toed boots slung over his shoulder. Fortunately, no one at the security area had thought to look inside his boots for contraband. We all knew that had been a close call. In spite of the pot adventures, all four of us felt we had enjoyed one of our best trips. One more trip with Matt, and then I'll move on.

Ensenada

Scott, Matt, my brother Bill and I went to an L.A. Raiders football game on October 31, 1983. After the game we decided to go to Ensenada, Mexico, and the four of us squeezed onto the bench seat of my pick-up for the ninety mile drive to Ensenada, Mexico.

Matt during our Ensenada adventure

We got to Ensenada a little after sundown. It was Halloween, and the town was beginning to party. We all decided to do a little shopping and pick up some souvenirs. I waited outside sitting on the truck fender and watching the festivities while Mat and Scott entered a shop. A short time later, they came out to hand me a paper sack and then went into the shop again. Curious, I unwrapped the object in the sack and found they had bought me a dildo. I looked up and saw two elderly women walking towards me. As they passed in front of me, I put the dildo between my legs and whistled. Wow! What a look!

Soon the boys came out with their purchases. Matt had bought a leather jacket, and Scott had got some cowboy boots and a twelve-inch wooden dildo.

As we walked along the street, I told the boys what I had done. We all laughed when I described the look the old ladies had given me. The town was really coming alive, and we enjoyed the noise, costumes, and general celebration. As we continued walking along, the boys began to play around with their new toy. Suddenly, a police car pulled up across the street. Matt saw them first and tried to hide the dildo in the gutter, but he was too late. The policemen came across the street and stopped us. We learned later that the two old ladies I had fooled around with had called the police department and lodged a complaint. Soon Matt, Scott and I were handcuffed and put in the back of their police car. My brother Bill was far enough behind us so that he didn't get caught; but he looked pretty unhappy as left him standing there to stare as we passed him in the police car on our way to jail.

I knew from experience that we were going to get fined. Since we were handcuffed, I couldn't reach my billfold, so I told Scott to reach around my back fish it out of my pocket, give me all the big bills, and leave only the singles. As it worked out, Scott couldn't see in the dark. Because it was so dark in the back seat of the Mexican patrol car, he couldn't tell the difference between the large and small bills, and he took out the small bills rather than the larger ones. When we got to the police station and took us inside, I felt like I was on the set of the TV show "Barney Miller." All the holding cells had bars on the front and the guys in jail could see what was going on at the front desk.

They brought us in, and all five of us stood at the rail at the front desk. There was only one woman behind the booking counter. Neither she or the policemen bringing us in spoke English. As the woman booking us typed out the charges, she stopped and pointed to the bags the policeman had confiscated were carrying. She obviously was asking to see the evidence, and they handed the bags to her. As she began unwrapping the dildo, we held our breath. When she saw it, she let out a little scream. We all tried not to laugh, but it was too funny, and all of us, including the cops, and the guys behind bars in the holding cell burst out laughing. However, we didn't laugh long. They fined us $500. I told them we only had enough money to get home. Of course, they fined us all the money we had and then let us go. As we walked back through town on our way back to my truck, people pointed and laughed at us. Scott had put a twenty in his watch pocket, and I had a few bucks in my boot.

We found Bill at my truck, and the four of us got out of Mexico.

Israel

In 1992, my son, Danny Mark, called and told me to call Bob, the head engineer at the Mirage Hotel. I called, made an appointment with him, and the next day I met Avi Nacush, one of five brothers who owned the Jordache jean company.

He told me that they were building a resort hotel in Eilat, Israel. He had noticed the Kooldeck around the swimming pool at the Mirage Hotel, and they wanted to use it on their pool in Eilat.

We had a short meeting, and they asked me if I would go to Eilat to teach their workers how to install Kooldeck. Of course, I was ready to go. However, I asked to take George, my best Kooldeck installer, with me. They agreed, and three days later we were on our way.

George and I flew to Tel Aviv, Israel. From there, we flew in a small company plane to Eilat.

Eilat is a resort town on the Red Sea, and we were put up in a hotel right at the water's edge. In addition to the lodging, we were each paid $400 per day. Although we were ready to work, the pool they were building was behind schedule and not yet ready to have the Kooldeck installed.

With free time on our hands, George and I toured Israel. We went to the old town of Jerusalem and then to the Dead Sea where I went swimming. I enjoyed floating like a cork in the dense salt water. On another tour, we went to Masada and then to Jericho.

Even after we had been in Eilat for two weeks, the pool still was not yet ready for our part of the work. Rather than to stay in Eilat, we decided to rent a car and take a trip to Cairo, Egypt. Driving across the Sinai Desert, we saw the small sand dunes made by destroyed Egyptian tanks, remnants of the six-day Israeli-Egyptian 1967 War, We could still see the tank gun turrets sticking up out of the sand dunes. Soon we went through the tunnel under the Suez Canal and entered Cairo. From Eilat to Cairo was only 430 km, or only about 260 miles, and it took us about five hours. In Cairo, we checked in at an old hotel where they gave us a room on the top floor.

We did all the touristy things. We spent a lot of time in the museum. Then we went to the Pyramids, rode camels and ate delicious food.

My ride at the Pyramids

Saturday morning George was awakened about 4:30 by a strange noise outside. He got up and opened the window. Then he awakened me to ask me about the noise. I got up and went to the window, and I still get goosebumps when I think about that sound. The sound came from thirteen million Moslems praying their morning prayer on their Sabbath. It was a high-pitched eerie sound, and it unnerved both of us. We were eager to get away from that sound and from that hotel. As we packed our bags we decided to take them with us on our tour to the Pyramids.

After eating breakfast at a restaurant near the Pyramids, we decided we had better get back to our job in Eilat. Since we had our overnight bags with us, we didn't go back to our hotel, but headed back to Eilat where they were expecting us that same day.

On the way back across the Sinai desert, a five hour trip turned into over the whole day. Our rental Ford broke down halfway across the desert, and by the time we were able to get help, contact the rental company, and find a way back to Eilat, we were a day late getting back. When we finally arrived the next morning, everyone hugged us, exclaiming how happy they were to see us safe and sound.

We couldn't understand why we were getting all this attention. Then our friends told us they were worried because there had been a large earthquake in Cairo. The hotel where we had stayed had been destroyed, and because we had not checked out, everyone thought we had been killed. The Nacush brothers in Eilat had even called my kids and told them we were dead. I quickly called home and told them what had happened. George and I were very happy we had left a day early.

Finally, after having been in Eilat for a month, George and I gave the workers a demonstration on how to install the Kooldeck, and then we collected our four-hundred dollars-a-day pay. Selling our finishing tools to a contractor, we left for home.

This trip to Israel would be my last trip to foreign lands. The restlessness was gone, but all the trips and all the foreign lands still had failed to fill the empty place in my heart.

Settled

Our house on Duneville Street

I returned to Vegas and decided to settle down. I owned a half acre on the outskirts of Vegas, and in 1993, I decided to build my dream house there.

At the time, my girlfriend Joannie and I decided to throw in together and build the kind of house we always wanted. We decided on a 3,000 square foot single story Spanish style house with a three-car garage on Duneville Street. We each sold our present homes to finance the new one. We had a saying: "Debt-free in '93, in the door in '94." We made our deadline and moved in in December 1994. It was a beautiful home; we both loved it, and we lived there until 2005. We married in 2000, and I worked on cleaning up financial legal clutters so we could live our lives with less complication.   Before moving back to Phoenix, we sold our place for $850,000.

When we got to Phoenix, we bought the first house we looked at. We paid $300,000 cash for the house where we still live.

Joannie and I married in 2016 for the second time.

Part II

Memories in My Heart

I have to live with myself and so

I want to be fit for myself to know

I want to be able as days go by

always to look myself straight in the eye;

I don't want to stand with the setting sun

and hate myself for the things I've done.

Edgar A Guest

Our Parents
Never Knew...

Watermelons

I got my first traffic ticket when I was twelve years old when I was in the watermelon business. As I have mentioned, my dad was in the trucking business, and we often had four or five pickups. My parents always went to bed early, and my fourteen-year-old sister, Bobbie-Lou and I would sneak out and push one of the trucks down the alley. One evening I started the truck and drove it down the alley to 10th Street. As soon as I turned on to the street, I saw the police car, and I knew I was caught. I stopped at the side of the road. The policeman walked up and gave me a ten-dollar ticket and a good talking to. My mother had to go to court to pay the ticket, and the judge said that if it happened again, I would go to jail.

As we grew older, and as our parents still went to bed early, Bill and I would sneak a truck out for whatever we needed to do. Eventually we used the truck to haul watermelons from an experimental watermelon field at Seventh Street and the north canal.

We knew whoever took care of that field never picked the melons, so we figured we weren't exactly stealing; and, for a few years, that field was our money tree. I had access to a truck and an unlimited supply of melons. My brother Bill and I would get a truckload of melons, and the guys in my neighborhood became my sales people. The deal was, "You guys sell one melon for a dime or three for a quarter, then we split 50-50. Two brothers, Austin and Billy Tuck were especially successful. Every year at watermelon season, they sold more melons than all the other guys put together. Through those years we developed several fields of melons. One year, when I was sixteen years old, a friend and neighbor, Eddie Aguirre's dad, had a farm where he raised watermelons. One evening, Eddie, Dwight Stubbs and I decided to go to Eddie's dad's farm and get a load of melons. I could legally drive by now. We went to my house and got a pickup, and then we drove to the farm to get a truckload of watermelons. Once the truck was loaded, we drove back to Eddie's place and started dividing up the melons.

It was evident that Dwight was taking the biggest and best melons. Once I made the mistake of asking Dwight why he thought he should get the best of the picking. I said, "It's my truck and Eddie's farm, so why should you get the best melons?" That's when Dwight hit me and knocked me out of the truck, and I suppose he thought that was a good answer. I agreed – silently --

and I didn't discuss it ever again. The next day, my best salesmen, the Tuck brothers were right there ready to start selling.

I had another source for watermelons. My Uncle Tex, Mom's brother, had two boys, Len and Buckey. They lived on a little farm in south Phoenix, and next to their farm was an irrigation ditch running along the edge of a watermelon field. To get the melons, a couple of us would go up the ditch about 150 yards, pick the melons and then throw them into the irrigation ditch to float down where the others would catch them by driving sticks into the water where it went through a culvert under the road. With the sticks stopping the melons, we would pluck them out of the water and put them in the truck. Splitting up the bounty, I would take mine home. Of course, the Tuck brothers were ready to go to work. This melon business went on for five or six years.

Twenty-five years later, when they came up to visit me and my family, I finally found out what made the Tuck brothers such good salesmen. We were reminiscing about the past when I asked them how they sold so many more watermelons than all the rest of us. They began to laugh. They said it was no secret. They sold the watermelons for twenty-five cents each instead of three for twenty-five cents. Instead of ten cents each, they got twenty-five cents.

Austin and Billy Tuck taught me a good lesson. By working smart, they were able to make more money during melon season than I did. Now, let me see, who were the really smart ones?

Shooting

When I was a kid we always had all kinds of shotguns, rifles, and pistols, and shooting formed a large part of our recreation. We would often get up early in the morning, pack up some food, and go out to the river-bottom or desert either to hunt, target shoot, or just to go "plinking." I still have the guns we used, and I have added many more. There are now about fifty firearms in my collection.

Every time I walk by the front of the gun cabinet I built in eighth grade, I see that hexagon rifle, or a favorite shotgun, and I remember the times when I would go dove-hunting with my Dad, and lie under the front of the truck waiting for the birds. I view the other rifles and shotguns my father touched, and they bring back treasured memories.

Some of the firearms I handled in my younger years bring back other kinds of memories, including memories of the times of the two people I shot and wounded.

I shot and wounded my first victim when I was in the seventh grade.

We weren't supposed to use the guns when my folks were gone, but we did. One day, when my folks were gone, I decided to take a .22 rifle and shoot at doves on the overhead power lines. Since I was shooting up in the air, I wasn't concerned about hitting anyone. The next morning my dad was reading the paper, and he slowly read out loud, "Man hit by a stray bullet while walking west near Ninth Street and Van Buren."

Immediately I knew it was I who shot him. Having no desire to get into any discussion about a falling bullet, I left the breakfast table pretty quickly.   I never confessed to my parents that I was the culprit, but I learned a most important lesson. I never again just shot a weapon without knowing where the bullet was going. What goes up must come down. I learned that the hard way.

The other person I shot was my brother. It happened when I was a senior in high school.   Bill and I decided to go deer hunting at Dugas Ranch about seventy-five miles north of Phoenix.   I accidentally shot

Bill in the calf of his leg. The bullet went through without hitting the bone. There was little blood, and I put a bandage on it. We didn't go straight home, but rather camped for the night. The next day, we decided not to go hunting but returned to Phoenix where I finally took Bill to the hospital. The people in the Emergency Room told us all gunshot wounds had to be reported to the police, and we gave them our story.

Because our mom was at home dying of cancer. We decided we didn't need to cause our family any additional trouble just because I had been stupid. I told Bill we had to lie about how he got shot.

We made up a story about us frog hunting in the creek that ran through our camp. We said a bullet ricocheted off a rock and hit him in the leg.

My dad believed us; the police bought our story, and that ended that. A short time later our story came out in the paper. It was years later before we told the truth.

This is how it really happened. I was upset with Bill. We had left camp before daylight and had spent the whole day hunting without success. We were with about ten other guys, and we had ridden up from Phoenix in a large World War II Army truck.   That morning, when we got to our hunting ground, they said we should all be at the truck at 6:00 P.M. We had a ways to go to get back to the truck, and I told Bill we had to get going, or they would leave us. However, Bill stopped and wouldn't move, no matter what I said. I finally left him standing there and walked about a hundred yards ahead of him. I stopped, looked back, and saw that he stubbornly had not moved a step. I knew the Mexicans we had hitched a ride with would leave us if we were late getting back to their truck so I decided I would make him move. Taking out my .22 pistol, I aimed next to him, and pulled the trigger. My aim was bad. The bullet went through his calf, and he sat down. I went back to get him, and I bandaged the wound. He got up, and we hiked back to the truck. That is the real story. The day after we got home, our story was in the newspaper.

Bill

Escape

After graduation from high school, I decided to go to college. While I was away during my first semester, Bill admitted himself to the state mental hospital to be treated for his schizophrenia. Concerned about my family, I traveled back and forth from Indiana to Phoenix six times over old Route 66. I drove two times and hitch-hiked four times.

The first time I came home to visit my brother was during the short Thanksgiving break. Next, I came for Christmas. The third time was spring break. Finally, the school year was over, and I headed for home.

When I got home in May, I found out Bill had run away from the hospital. We searched, but we could not find a clue as to where he had disappeared.

When we did find Bill, he said they gave him shock treatments which he hated, and he had run away. Escape hadn't been difficult. He wasn't in a secure ward, so he simply had walked out of the hospital and had hitched a ride with a truck driver.

Several hours later, someplace in New Mexico, the truck driver told him to get out. Bill was not a talker, and the driver needed someone to talk to in order to keep him awake.

Bill didn't care where he was going; he simply wanted to get as far away from the hospital as he could, so he headed east. His next ride let him out in St. Louis.

He had only had forty-dollars when he left Phoenix, and now he was cold, hungry, and broke. Somehow he found a homeless shelter where he was able to get fed and have a bed for the night. The next morning, he found his way to the railroad tracks where he met some hoboes who told him how and where he could hop a train going east.

Bill found a place to hop on a train, and he spotted one grinding slowly along the tracks. Running alongside the train, he grabbed hold of a moving box-car and was yanked off his feet. Knees dragging, he held on for dear life until finally he was able to pull himself up onto the floor of the boxcar.

By now he decided to go to New York. He got off the train in Raleigh, North Carolina, and he was cold. Figuring he would be even colder in New York, he changed his mind and decided to go to Miami, Florida, instead. He jumped out of the box-car and headed for a highway to hitch a ride heading south.

Caught

Bill was dirty from the train ride, and he needed to wash his clothes. He started walking, and after some time, he saw a farm with a big barn. He went into the barn and found what he thought was a bar of soap. After washing his clothes and resting for a while, he was back hitch-hiking on the road. He went through Mobile, Alabama, Mississippi, and ended up outside of Pensacola, Florida. Throughout the trip he learned how to find shelters for food and sleeping space. Sometimes he ate with hobos and slept rough in the open. For a seventeen-year-old kid, that journey taught him a lot about life.

It wasn't long into his journey when he discovered he had made a mistake when he had washed his clothes. It wasn't a bar of soap he had used; it was a bar of lye, and his clothes were falling apart. In rags, he continued hitch-hiking across Florida.

Finally, he came up over a hill on the outskirts of a town near Pensacola, and he saw a large house. As he watched, he saw a man come out of the house, get into his car, and drive off. Bill's clothes were falling apart, and he was cold and hungry. Bill decided to see what he could find to eat and wear inside that house. Reaching the house, he found the back door was open. Quietly he entered and made sure no one else was there. Then he went into the kitchen and ate. After eating, he went into the master bedroom. The closet was full of clothes. Getting out of his rags, he took some clothes from the closet and put them on. The clothes were a bit too big, but they would do.

After dressing, he went through the night stand and found a gold watch and two guns. The .22 was loaded, and the .38 was empty. He put the watch and the .38 in the pocket of his new coat.

Needing money, Bill planned to hock the watch and pistol. Before leaving the house, he stole a sack full of food. Walking back out to the road, he hitched a ride to Jacksonville, Florida.

Reaching Jacksonville, as Bill walked down a street looking for a pawn shop, two policemen approached and asked him where he was going. He told them, "Miami."

Because he must have looked a bit suspicious in his ill-fitting clothes, the police searched him and found the stolen gun and the watch.

Knowing the jig was up, Bill confessed. They took him back to Pensacola where he went to court. The judge sentenced Bill to three years in Rayford Prison, one of the worst prisons in the country. It came out later that the house Bill had chosen to break into belonged to the same judge that tried and sentenced Bill to Rayford prison.

Bill was put on the chain gang. He told us later that it was just like the movie, "Cool Hand Luke." After a few weeks, he'd had enough and confessed that he was a runaway from a mental hospital in Phoenix, Arizona.

After the authorities had checked out his story, they moved him into the hospital where he stayed for about two weeks. Two men then escorted him back to Phoenix. By that time, Bill was more than ready to go home.

Hunting and Horses

Horses

As a kid, the one thing I always wanted was a horse. However, when we moved into the city to the Garfield place, of course, I couldn't have my own horse.

My cousins, still living out in the country, they all had horses.

One day, when I was eight years old, my family was visiting my dad's brother, and my dad asked if I wanted to sit on my Uncle's big white horse. You bet I did. My dad picked me up and sat me on the horse's back. Because the horse had no saddle or bridle, I grasped his mane to hold on. Suddenly, something spooked the horse, and he took off running.

I held on for dear life. Abruptly, the horse stopped, lowered his head, and I went flying. When I landed I broke both of my arms. My mother's sister, Aunt Effie, came over to inspect the damage. She told my dad to get some wooden splints. At first I didn't know what she was going to do. She took my arm and yanked on it to set it straight. Then she took the splint and secured it on my wrist. I let out a yell. Then she did the same thing to my other arm. That lasted until they took me to the doctor to get my casts. Two weeks after the casts came off, I fell out of a tree and broke my arm again.

In the years following, I had many encounters with horses. Once I entered a little rodeo in Veyo, Utah, and rode a little bull and a horse. I broke my ribs that time. Another time I raced a horse that Bud Penton, my boss at that time, was boarding. I didn't know that horse had been barred from racing because he would run through fences. As I turned the horse to head home, he broke into a run, and I couldn't get him to stop. Unable to make the turn into Bud's place, the horse slipped and fell into the five-strand barbed wire fence. I flew over the fence and landed in Bud's front yard. The poor horse was all tangled in the fence and couldn't get up. Getting up, I found I didn't break anything this time, and I ran to get Bud. He got some wire cutters, and we untangled the horse which had some cuts and scratches but no real injuries. I never rode that horse again. But I still loved to ride.

In 1970, my son Danny and I went to Missoula, Montana to hunt elk with my friend Paul Grube, a pool plasterer. His father, his son, and other friends completed the party. We had rented a cabin with corrals for the horses.

The second morning, I rode out alone. After about an hour, I got off my horse to get a drink. Something spooked my horse, and he ran off and left me. I decided I had better start walking. It would be a long one.

When the riderless horse got back to our camp, Grube and his bunch had already left, and my twelve-year-old son, Danny was frightened and alone.

When I finally got back to camp, Danny wasn't there, and my Ford Bronco was gone. It had snowed the night before, and I could see from the tire tracks of my Bronco that Danny had gotten in, made a wide turn, had run over some big rocks, and crossed the bridge over the creek to go out to the road. He told me later he had gone to get help. At one spot, trying to turn around, he had gotten stuck. Somehow, he turned the locks on the front hubs to the four-wheel drive setting and got out.

The next morning Danny and I went hunting together. After being out for about two hours, we heard six or eight shots from somewhere on a hill up above us. I finally saw the shooter. He was dressed in red. At first we couldn't see what he was shooting at. After he shot a couple more times, we finally saw his target -- a small herd of cows that had been missed and left behind in the fall round-up. Lying down behind a dead tree, we hid ourselves and watched that crazy hunter in red. If he knew we had seen him shoot the cow, well, I wasn't taking any chances. The shooter in red finally figured out what he was shooting at, and left.

After the hunter got out of sight Danny and I went over to the little herd of cows. Two were dead. One was shot in the stomach and in the leg. The rest of the little herd just milled around. I told Danny I had to shoot the wounded cow. He began to cry, and I joined him in shedding tears as we well knew what had to happen. I shot the wounded cow. I think that is when I decided I had had enough of hunting and killing things.

The cows had brass bands on their ears identifying the name of the ranch that owned the little herd. When we arrived back at camp, everyone else was out hunting, Leaving Danny at the camp to tell the others what had happened, I drove about fifty miles to the cattle ranch identified by the bands on the cows' ears.

When I got to the ranch, the owner and cowhands were all ears as I told my story and described where the cattle were. It didn't take long for the angry cowboys to load their ponies into trucks. They asked if I wanted to go with them, and. I immediately accepted. They loaded a horse for me, and then we were off.

We drove as far as we could and then mounted up. When we got to the herd, they were still there where I had left them.

I had no idea what I was getting myself into. Immediately the cow ponies took charge. All I had to do was hang on. The ranch-hands rounded up the cows and started them towards home. That round-up and cattle drive was one of the most exciting things I have ever done, and it was all I could do to stay on the horse. When a cow broke from the herd, I held on for dear life as my horse chased it. What a ride that was. I didn't know if the horse was going to zig or zag around trees, boulders and dead logs. Would the horse jump or go around? Sometimes I would be almost out of the saddle and up on the horse's neck.

The cow ponies were amazing. In and out, over or under, stop or go around. It was all up to the horse. This ride went on for about four hours. Finally, we got the cows back to the little corral. When I got off my horse, for a little while, I couldn't walk. The cowboys laughed at me and said I was a tenderfoot. Yes, and I was saddle sore for the next few days. And no, I would not like to wrangle cows for a living.

Last Hunt

One of the biggest changes in my life came when I was about forty years old. Up until then, I had hunted all my life. I had killed deer, wild pigs, antelope, elk, bobcat, and at one time, I killed the largest mountain lion in North America. I killed duck, doves, quail, rabbits, squirrels, rattlesnakes, Gila monsters, foxes, frogs and fish. To my shame, I was indifferent to the fact that I was killing just for the excitement of hunting. I got sort of a selfish satisfaction that I had the power to do so. That all changed the last time I went elk hunting.

The change came on a hunting trip to Rifle, Colorado. I was with a party of other hunters and guides, and we had perched on a hill overlooking a migration route the elk used. The hunters shot at the animals from long range. Frequently missing the kill shot, and only wounded the animal, they would watch indifferently as the suffering beast staggered out of range of their high-powered rifles. Rather than track the animal to finish the kill, they simply shot another in the herd within range. They wounded elk after elk and let them run off to suffer and die slowly. They made no attempt to track it and put it out of its pain. Shot after shot, elk after elk. I got sick. Then, it was as if a switch got flicked to the "off" position inside me. That day my desire to hunt died with the wounded elk. I never hunted again. I ask forgiveness all the time for the damage I did with a gun.

Now, instead of hunting animals, I feed the rabbits, the quail, the doves and the little birds of all kinds. Love for all animals has replaced my indifference. I will never harm them again.

Angry Women

Rosa

It was September 1961. Ted Stubbs, Pat Shaughnessy and I decided to go dove hunting. Ted drove and Pat sat in the in the front seat on the passenger side. I sat in the back seat with our shotguns.

At about 35th Avenue and Indian School Road, I looked over and saw Rosa, my ex-stepmother. I picked up my double barreled 20 gauge L.C. Smith shotgun and told Ted to pull up right alongside of her car. I intended to get her attention and then point my shotgun at her.

I knew it was wrong, but at that time I didn't care. As Ted pulled next to her car, Rosa looked over and saw me. She didn't panic like I thought she would. Actually, she pulled over to the side of the road and stopped. Ted pulled right in behind her.

I got out of Ted's car and walked around to her driver's side. I said, "Do you remember me?" To my surprise, she began screaming obscenities at me. She had a pencil in her hand and tried to write down Ted's license plate number. I grabbed the pencil. Then, still screaming obscenities at me, she started getting out of her car.

Our two cars had stopped in front of a used car lot. People began to look at us. I retreated to our car with Rosa in hot pursuit. I tumbled into the front seat, and she tried to come in after me. I couldn't close the car door because, clawing and punching me, she was halfway into our car. Wanting to scare her, I told Ted to take off so we would drag her down the street. I was only kidding, but Ted took me seriously.

Pulling out, he sideswiped Rosa's car and pinned her between the two vehicles, but Ted didn't stop. Still

screaming, Rosa was still half in our car. Ted didn't stop.
I tried as hard as I could to hold Rosa up so her knees
wouldn't drag on the pavement.

Finally, after about a hundred yards, she had quit
screaming and was holding on for dear life. Ted
stopped. I turned her loose, and as she stood there, I
reached over and snatched her glasses, crunched them
in my hand, and threw them into the road. Then we
took off and left her standing there.

We didn't go hunting that day, for we sort of
thought we might be the hunted instead. Did anyone
get our license number? Were the police after us? We
heard nothing until the next morning. The story in the
paper read, "Hoodlums attack seventy-five year old
woman in broad daylight." Rosa didn't mention my
name in the article. However, two days later I got a
subpoena to appear in court.

I knew I was in real trouble and might even go to
jail so I hired one of the best attorneys in Phoenix to

defend me. On the day of my arraignment, I happened to get in an elevator with Rosa's attorney. Though we had never met before, he knew who I was and let me know what he thought of me. He said guys like me should be in Vietnam or in jail. Of course, that shook me a bit. Then, as I entered the courtroom, I saw Rosa with attorneys from Atlas Van Lines and her witnesses. On my side were Ted, my aunt, my two sisters, my attorney Bob Begam, and me. I had told Bob the story about what happened. Rosa's lawyers went first. They presented their side of the encounter with Rosa and my meddling with her and my dad and Atlas Van Lines. Then they rested their case.

It was now our turn. Nothing had been said about the guns. Bob said he was not going to put me on the stand. No one was to mention the guns.

This time Bob told the court our side of the story. He told the story this way: "Danny, this fine young Christian, had come home from Bible college to find his father was married. The marriage lasted four months. Danny's father had only gone to school until the third grade. No education. Didn't really know what he was signing. However, she got half of the corporation." When Bob finished his part, he then told the story of our encounter with Rosa. He said we saw Rosa stopped on the side of the road. We saw her and pulled in behind her. When she saw it was me, she attacked me. She was cursing and acting like a crazy person.

After my attorney finished telling my story, the judge told Rosa she should be ashamed of herself. She had caused enough trouble and the judge dismissed all her charges. Yes, I felt very fortunate to have had a great attorney. I never saw or heard tell of Rosa again.

Maggie

By 1971, about two months after Diana had taken our kids had moved to Phoenix, I was doing some pool work at Wayne Newton's ranch on the outskirts of Vegas. His next door neighbor saw me working, and she came over to tell me she needed some pool work done. I stopped over and bid her job, and she asked me when I could start. That's how I met Maggie.

One hot afternoon while I was working on her pool, Maggie invited me into her house to have a cold drink, and after that she seduced me. Although she was about ten years older than I, we spent a lot of time together. Maggie was very rich and had just divorced her husband, the State Treasurer at the time. I didn't know where she had got her money. Anyway, she had a large motorhome, and we traveled to the Grand Canyon and other interesting spots in our State.

One day Maggie asked me if I thought my ex-wife would take our kids for a million dollars. Wow, I wasn't ready for that one. Of course, I said, "No way."

Maggie kept trying to get me to move in with her, but I absolutely refused, and suddenly the whole romance came to an abrupt end. The day that happened, Maggie had been drinking her Grande Marnier and had gotten sloppy drunk. She then told me this incredible story about how she got her money.

She had been married to Trader Bill, the owner Trader Bill's, an established store in downtown Las Vegas. He had also owned about half of the block. Bill was crippled and confined to a wheel chair. She told me that Bill was sick, but he just wouldn't die. Tired of waiting, Maggie decided to take matters into her own hands. One day, after they had consumed a few drinks, she took him outside in his wheelchair and pushed him into their swimming pool to drown.

I had always suspected Maggie was a little nuts, but I was a young man having a great fling with a rich woman who wanted me as a companion. I suddenly realized she wasn't a just little nuts; she was crazy.

Deciding I was done with her, I stayed away for a few days while I struggled with what I should do. During this time, Maggie kept calling, and when I didn't answer, she finally came by my house to look for me; but Matt was the only one home. Finally, one morning, I decided "to take the bull by the horns" and tell her it was over.

I was a bit spooked as I drove into her long driveway. When I got out of my Bronc, Maggie invited me into the house. I went in, but I didn't sit down, and I started to tell her that it was over. As I was talking, she pulled out a .38 revolver and pointed it at my head. I saw her pull the hammer back, and a live round rolled into the chamber. I told her I thought we were just having fun together, and if I had ever led her on, that wasn't my intention. After that, I told her I was going to leave.

I went out and got into my Bronco, but it wouldn't start. I got out and opened the hood. Maggie's handyman had pulled all the spark-plug wires out of the motor. I definitely didn't want to go back into the house and face her holding that gun again, so I started walking down her long driveway. I shouted back to her that I was going to call the police. The muscles in my back tightened with the fear of a .38 round slamming into me.

Reaching a pay-phone, and instead of calling the police, I called Matt to come to pick me up. When he arrived, we drove to the auto supply and got some new plug wires for my Bronco, and then we went back to retrieve it.

When I had left Maggie's place earlier that morning, the big iron gate at the entrance had been locked, but now it was open. We drove up the driveway, stopped beside my Bronco, and opened the hood. The wires already had been replaced. I got in and it started right up. We didn't lose any time leaving. After we left those big iron gates behind, I never saw or heard from Maggie again.

Close Calls

Vandercheck's Furniture

In 1955, The Vondercheck family who were members at the First Missionary Church, had a cabin in Greer, Arizona, and they needed some furniture delivered to it. I had been to their cabin the summer before and knew the way there. Seeing an opportunity to do some turkey-hunting, I arranged with the Vanderchecks to take the furniture up for them, and that would give me and my friends, Sonny Gillam and John Wilmouth, a chance to go turkey hunting. We loaded John's pickup with the furniture that morning. We had to play in a church softball game that evening so it was about ten o'clock before the three of us took off.

John and Sonny were big guys, both about six feet six inches tall, and I was squeezed between them on the single bench seat.   John drove. We had gone through the switchbacks in Salt River Canyon and had set out on to the Indian Reservation road. About two o'clock in the morning John told us he was getting sleepy. We stopped so Sonny could take over. Sonny had been driving for about a half-hour when we came to a fork in the road. Sonny started going straight, but John told him to turn left. Sonny tried to swerve to the left, but it was too late. We skidded sideways, turned over and tumbled down an embankment to land upside down in a large ravine. The motor was still running, and John hollered for Sonny to turn off the engine, but Sonny was unconscious. I reached up and turned off the engine. I smelled gasoline running into the truck cab.

The truck was upside down, and the three of us were trapped in the front seat We were in a ravine, and we couldn't open the doors. Jammed between those two big guys, except for the knots on the top of my head, I wasn't hurt. I wriggled out through the broken windshield and looked up toward the highway to see maybe thirty Indians standing at the roadside looking down at us.

I motioned for some help. They saw our predicament, and about eight of them came down to give us a hand. We all got on one side and rolled the truck back on all four wheels. The guys got out of the truck. We all had bumps, bruises and cuts, but they were all minor. John checked the oil. It was low, but the truck would still run. Then John got behind the wheel, started the engine, and the rest of us pushed to finally got the battered truck back up on the road.

Looking around, we eventually found all the goods that had been in the back of the truck scattered all over the embankment.   The furniture was a complete loss. We loaded what little we could find, and then went on our way. After our adventure, John decided he was awake enough to drive again while Sonny and I sat with our feet sticking out through the empty windshield frame. Because of the occasional chips of glass flying back at us, we had to keep our eyes closed.

We didn't get any turkeys that year.

Ditch Day

An early close call was on senior ditch day in 1956. Our class had gone to Oak Creek Canyon in northern Arizona and a few of us decided to climb up the red rock cliffs. We all got part way up when Frances Wilcox became frightened and wanted to go back down. Jimmy Patterson and I volunteered to help her. I went first, then Jim and Frances. As I was going down, I stumbled, fell and slipped over the edge of an outcropping.   It was hundreds of feet straight down. As I fell, I can remember thinking, "I'm ready to go." Then I hit something and got knocked out.

When I woke up, I found myself on a small ledge about eight feet down from where I had started, and I was pinned to the ledge by a prickly pear cactus. Jimmy got a limb and helped me back up. We all got down okay. However, with cactus in all my private parts, it was a long ride home, and sitting in that car seat was agony; but at least I was alive.

Lost

Another close call occurred 1972 while I was on a hunting trip with Paul Grube in Montana. I got lost.

Having left Paul with the truck, I decided to track an elk through waist deep snow. Concentrating on the tracking, I paid little attention to where I was going or even how much time had passed. I never realized I was lost until I paused at a spot where the tracks of my elk got lost in the mix of a bunch of other elk tracks. I was alone, very scared, and very hungry. Although I wasn't sure of my directions, I started back along the way I thought I had come. After a time I heard Grube sounding the horn on his truck, and I started to move toward the sound. Then, sometime later, I heard the horn again, but this time it came from a different direction. I changed my path to go toward the new sound. This happened several times. I was becoming more frightened and more fatigued. Finally, after nine hours, I found my way back to Grube. He confessed that when he had got no response from me in one spot, he had moved to another, and then another. I couldn't be angry with him. I was just too tired and too hungry.

Stuck

The next close call with death came in 1980 when the Arnolds invited us to a swimming party. Their swimming pool was about twenty yards from the house. When the Arnolds called us in to eat, everyone left the pool except me. I was on the diving board, and I decided to dive through the middle of the small life saver floating in the middle of the pool. I dove, and my head and upper arms went through the ring, but the rest of me was stuck. It was like being lassoed with my arms pinned at my side and head held under water. I knew I was in real trouble. Everyone had already gone into the house, and I was alone. With my arms and head firmly held under water. I tried not to panic. I realized my only chance to survive was to get to the shallow end of the pool, so I began kicking, not knowing in which direction I was moving. I kicked and prayed that I was headed towards the shallow end. I couldn't hold my breath much longer. Finally, my toes touched the break in the pool. Thank God, I was moving in the right direction. I found myself in the shallow water. I kept on kicking. As the pool sloped upward, my feet found the bottom, but I still couldn't raise my head out of the water. It was pinned to my chest. At last I got to the edge of the pool and somehow rolled out of the pool onto the deck. I had made it out alive. It's sort of funny as I now reflect on that incident. I came about as close to dying as anyone can. I lay there until I could gather myself together enough to go to join my friends. No one in the party ever knew how close I came to drowning.

Whirlpool

My next brush with death came in 1984. Our family had rented a motorhome and we had gone on a trip to the Northwest.   Stopping for the night to set up camp by the Rogue River, I decided to join the kids to swim. Swimming out further than the kids, I got caught in the swift current. The next thing I knew I was trapped in a giant whirlpool and was swirled round and round. I fought and struggled until I was totally exhausted, but I couldn't break out. The river had won. I quit struggling and gave up.

Shortly after this picture,
I almost drowned in a whirlpool.

The river must have thought it was no longer fun playing with me and decided to spit me out. On my back and barely able to keep my face and nose above water, I floundered to the shore and lay on the warm sand and thanked God for my deliverance.

Flying Pie

Back in the 1990s, I received a phone call and learned that Margie Erbe's fourteen-year-old son, Danny, had been killed while roller-blading.

With about 1,000 people in attendance, his funeral was a giant affair. After the funeral, about fifty of us were invited to the Erbes' home for refreshments. I visited with old friends, and then I went into the dining room with six others to get some dessert.   As I introduced myself to Pastor Mark, the preacher who had assisted in the funeral, a slice of cherry pie flew off the table and landed on the carpeted floor about six feet from the dessert table. Everyone in the room was shocked into silence. No one spoke. We just stood there, speechless and staring at the slice of pie.

Not believing what we had seen, and too shocked to speak, we looked at each other and then back at the pie. As we stared at the pie on the carpet, Margie's husband, Gale, came into the room. Seeing the cherry pie splattered on the long-nap white carpet, he turned and left and soon came back with some cleaning equipment, set it down by the cherry pie, and left.

Up to this point no one had said a word. I figured Margie's husband expected someone to clean up the mess, so I went over, got a rag and soap and started to clean up the pie. At that moment, Gale came back into the room and told me in no uncertain terms to stop and then asked what had happened.

I tried to think of something believable. The man had just buried his son. I could not say, "Gale, the pie just flew off the table." Finally, I looked up at him and told him that a little boy had dropped his piece of pie. No one in the room corrected me. We were all still stunned into silence. The six people in the room were

Jerry and Nancy Simmons, Georglyn, Beulah, myself and Pastor Mark who is pastor at Calvary Chapel here in Phoenix.

As I think back about that incident with the pie, I have no idea what made it happen. None of us do. However, I think about it often. I guess there are some things we will never understand.

Busted

Judge Seymour Brown

I had received a speeding ticket and was sitting in the courtroom. It was my first year in Vegas, 1963.

The judge, Seymour Brown, called my name and asked me to stay after court. When we met, he asked if I was in the pool business and if I knew his pool builder, Johnny Fertilla.

"Yes," I told him, "I've worked for all the pool builders in Vegas." He then told me he had some problem with his tile and Kooldeck. I agreed to take a look at his pool. The next day I went to his house and spent about one hour repairing his tile and Kooldeck.

For the next fifteen years I never paid another traffic citation. The judge would turn traffic tickets into parking tickets, and I would pay five dollars.

Having the judge as a friend paid continual dividends. My son, Matt, had received yet another traffic ticket bringing his collection of unpaid citations to more than $3,000. When Matt told me he was in trouble. I told him to call Judge Brown. He made an appointment to see the judge, and when he went into the judge's office, the judge had Matt's file before him. Judge Brown told Matt he ought to throw him in jail. After a strong lecture, he handed Matt his case file and told Matt to give it to his secretary on his way out. Leaving the judge's chambers, Matt went to the secretary's office, but no one was there. The Judge had handed Matt all his records. As Matt walked out of her office, he simply dropped the folder, fat with his file, into the trash bin. He never heard anything more from the court or from the judge.

Judge Gang, 1971

In 1971 Diane and I were giving an early evening reception for a friend at Red Rock Church. It was early evening. I went out front looking for my son Danny and his uncle, Pat, who was about the same age.

I saw the boys coming to the house. As they arrived, a police car pulled up and two cops got out, and one of the cops started yelling at them. The boys had a Red Rider BB gun with them, and it seemed they had shot out someone's window. The one cop was out of control. He started screaming obscenities and told them they were going to jail.

I intervened and told the boys to get in the house. The screaming cop started to grab Danny, and I told the boys to run. They ran, and I went with them. As I got to the front door of the house, the cop caught me. I dragged him into my house and grabbed hold of the upstairs railing. Both cops tried to get me loose, but I wouldn't let go.

In the middle of all this commotion, members of our church started to arrive to our reception. My wife was screaming for me to let go. However, I already knew this cop was nuts, and I wasn't about to. Finally, the cops Maced me and then hit me with their batons. Finally,I had to let go, and they handcuffed me.

As we went out my front door, the bad cop yanked on my arm and clamped the handcuffs much tighter. When they dragged me to the cop car I wouldn't get in. They Maced me again, and I still wouldn't get in the car. By now many more people began arriving. I saw my pastor, my Sunday school teacher, and many more of my friends. Finally, the cop slammed my head on top of the squad car. I decided I had better get in.

As I sat in the cop car I saw more police arrive. One of the officers came over to look in the back seat, and I began telling him what happened. I was shocked when he told me I was lucky it wasn't him because he would have beat the xxx out of me. When we drove off, I was beside myself with anger. I yelled at the cops to stop the car and take off the handcuffs.

"Please, Please stop the car," I tantalized them. I felt I could whip them both. Even if I got hurt, Oh how I wanted to get my hands on them. Of course, they had some mean comments for me as well. However, I told them they couldn't hurt me because too many people had seen my condition when we left my house.

When we arrived at the police station, my eyes burned, my nose was bleeding, and my head hurt like blazes. As I stood at the booking desk, I asked for something to clean my face with. That request was ignored. I asked for a drink. No response. Finally, they put me in a cell and told me to take my clothes off. I stood there considering their request. I told them no, I wasn't taking my clothes off. Just then I heard someone yell, "Do we have a Robert Daniel Henderson in custody?" Yes, was the reply. "Release him on Judge Gang's order." Wow, what a change in how I was treated. A nurse came and patched up the cuts on my head. They asked if I wanted something to drink and they brought me a cold drink. Then they released me.

The next day I called George Cromer, my friend and attorney. He said I could and should sue the city. So I did. At the arraignment the prosecutor said they would drop the charges against me if I would drop my charges. They had charged me with drunk and disorderly, resisting arrest, and assaulting an officer. At that time I was also divorcing my wife and really didn't need to complicate my life and further. I prayed and asked the Lord to guide me. At last, I decided to take their deal and decided not to sue.

A week or so later I was at the hospital to visit my brother-in-law. As I stepped into the elevator, standing right beside me was the bad cop. I looked at him and he looked at me. However, we didn't speak.

A few months later I found out that the out-of-control policeman got busted for some misdeed and then got fired from the police force. But my troubles weren't over. Somehow, the city failed to drop their charges against me. Because I threatened to sue again, the city finally got it straightened out and the charges against me were dropped.

Pot

In 1963, I smoked my first marijuana joint. It was with Ernst Wingert, a black man who worked for me. We both got stoned. I went home and told Diana, and she became so angry and upset that I got high that I never smoked pot again as long as we were married.

After my divorce, two guys from church, Floyd North and Russell Erby, had some marijuana, and we drove to Lake Mead. On the way, we smoked pot and listened to music. After we left the lake I learned by experience what the munchies were.   We stopped at a Burger King and ordered a Whopper and fries. That was the best hamburger and fries I had ever eaten. After that day, I smoked pot on a regular basis, but only after work and on weekends.

During this time, I had made friends with a man named, Tom Logan, who told me he had been one of the members on the original "Whiz Kids" radio and television programs. He taught a night-school class at UNLV , and that stirred my curiosity. Just for fun, I signed up just to see what kind of teacher he was. I don't even remember what the class was about.

Logan had just gotten a divorce, and he said he had some money he wanted to invest. We talked about it and we decided to invest together in some marijuana.

I got on the phone and asked around for information. I had only smoked for about a year; but I had developed some contacts, and I got in touch with a friend in Phoenix. A few days later, I got in touch with the guy who had the pot. Logan and I drove to Phoenix where I made another phone call and arranged a time and place for us to meet. I said I wanted my friend from Phoenix to be there. We planned to buy $12,000 worth of weed. With that much money, we had to be as careful as possible. When we all met at a park, I didn't know it then, but Logan had a pistol. We parked next to the car and opened our trunk. The other guy did the same. We gave them the money, and they gave us a bale of pot. I never did that again. I knew we might have been robbed, or killed.

That winter I went to Hawaii and found another source for marijuana. It was simple. I found two gay guys who said they could supply all I wanted. The cost was $2,000 a pound. After I got back to Vegas, I ordered one pound. A few days later the pot arrived via Federal Express. The next time I ordered two pounds. We never ordered more than two pounds because there is a federal law that states anyone who is caught with more than a kilo would lose their house or car or boat. A kilo is two and a quarter pounds. Everything went okay, and we waited for the two pounds. Finally it arrived in a delivery by Federal Express. My son Matt, and his girlfriend, got one pound of the shipment, and he left to take it over to my brother-in-law. I left my pound of pot sitting on a table and decided to take a shower.

A few minutes later, as I stepped out of the shower, my doorbell rang. I slipped into my blue jeans, andwent to answer the door. When I opened it, two policemen with drawn guns faced me. I had a pit bull that started to growl, I said, "Please don't shoot my dog."

My pit-bull, Dax

They entered, handcuffed me, and then sat me down on the floor. I didn't know it then, but Matt and his girlfriend, with their pound of pot, had also been stopped right after they had left my house. The excuse the police gave for the traffic stop was the claim that Matt's truck had a tail light out. When Matt learned the police were headed for my house, he told them I had a pit bull and, ". . . please don't shoot my dad's dog."

I sat on the floor as the cops searched my house. Of course, they found the pot.

While looking for the pot, the police also found guns everywhere. I had about fifty pistols and rifles hidden all over my house, and the cops thought they had caught a pot-smoking gun-runner. In Vegas I was required to register all my handguns, and they were all legal; but the cops didn't know that at the time. In their search, one of the cops did steal my favorite pocket knife. What worried me was that on my desk I also had $5,000 in one-hundred-dollar bills stacked at the bottom of my box of checks. Fortunately, they didn't find the money, but I didn't know that at that time.

As I sat handcuffed on the floor, I told the police the guns were all registered. The cops told me to shut up. Finishing their search, they loaded up my pot, my guns, and me into their patrol car. I asked if I could put on a jacket and was told it wouldn't be cold. I told them that I was already cold, that I had just got out of the shower when they came to the door, and that I had only a tee shirt and blue jeans on. They ignored me. I argued with them. I told them I had a physical problem and that if I got chilled, I could go into a severe chill that might kill me. They could not have cared less.

I said to one cop, "You would like for me to make a run for it so you could legally put a bullet in the back of my head. You hate me because I smoke pot. However, when you leave here you can go to the 7-11 and get your beer."

I continued to plead for a jacket, but my requests fell on deaf ears.

They took me to jail. It was on a Saturday night, and the jail holding room was full of drunks and lawbreakers, and it was very cold in the holding room.

I knew I was in trouble. I walked to the only door and beat on it. A woman finally came to the window in the door and told me to quit kicking the door. I told her it was too cold. She told me the thermostat was stuck and she couldn't do anything about it. I sort of panicked. What was I going to do? I beat on the door again. Finally the woman came back and pulled down the shade to cover the window on the holding-room door.

I was really cold. All I had on was a tee shirt and jeans and not even underwear. I finally went over to the bench that circled the room and sat down between two guys. It was a little better, but I was still in trouble. Seated there, I began to shiver uncontrollably. My head was bowed, and my eyes were closed when suddenly a warm heavy black leather coat was draped over me. I looked up, and a big man with a large beard hovered above me. I was shivering so bad I couldn't talk. He said, "I think you need this more than me." I was saved!

The next morning I called my daughter, Lois, and I told her our situation. Matt and I, and his girlfriend, Vickey, needed $3500 to make bail. Lois went to my house and looked in my box of checks. My $5,000 was still there. Thank you, Lord.

With the necessary money, Lois went to a bail bondsman friend of mine, and they bailed us out. As we were leaving the jail, Vickey's ex-boyfriend walked up behind Matt, and tapped him on the shoulder. When Matt turned around, he hit Matt in the mouth, knocking out his front teeth. We turned around and went back into the police station. The officer at the desk told us to get out because Matt was bleeding all over the floor. Matt and I went into the bathroom.

Matt had braces, and when he looked in the mirror and saw his teeth hanging, caught in his braces, he fell to his knees and began to shout, "Dad, he knocked my front teeth out."

It was about seven o'clock on a Sunday morning. I took Matt to the hospital, but they said there was nothing they could do. Next, we called Matt's dentist. When we got to his office, the dentist told us, while he couldn't help, even though it was Sunday morning, he would call another dentist friend.

That other dentist agreed to see Matt and told us to come to his office to see what he could do. When we got there, after a brief examination, the dentist started working. I was amazed at what that dentist was able to do. He took out Matt's braces and then reset his teeth back in his mouth. After reseating Matt's teeth, he replaced the braces. I was impressed with the first-class work this dentist did, and he only charged me $200.

Later, in court, Matt told the judge what had happened. The judge said it must not have been very serious because the doctor only charged $200. However, Matt didn't lose any of his teeth. Thank God!

Then it was my day in court. I pleaded guilty to possession of a controlled substance with intent to sell. The judge sentenced me to seven years in prison. My knees buckled, but I remained standing. He then commuted my sentence to one hundred hours of community service and then two years of probation.

My community service was at an old folks' rest home. When I went to see the facility, I was delighted to see they had a swimming pool. I learned the owners worked at the mental health hospital, and I made an appointment to see them.

When we met I told them my situation. I told them I could empty bedpans, go shopping, take old people for a walk, or better yet, I could repair the tile and coping and deck on their pool. It was a no-brainer. They gladly chose the alternative of my repairing their pool.

A few days later I drove to the retirement home to start my repairs. I had my Skillsaw, my extension cord, and my hammer and chisel. I went into the main building to get the key for the pool gate. Inside, I saw a long line of old people waiting patiently to get their medications.

Joining the slow line, I finally got my turn and asked the woman behind the desk for the pool key. She began to interrogate me. Did I have any experience? I told her I worked for all the pool companies in Vegas. Then she asked if I knew Jim Johnson. I said, "Yes, I know Jim." She asked what I thought of him. I said, "He is a good-for-nothing thief and liar." Then she told me he was her husband. I said, "That's your problem." She told me I would have to come back because she had to check out my story.

Disgusted and angry, I stalked out, climbed over the pool fence and started to work. A few minutes later, she came out and handed me the phone. It was Beverly, my probation officer. She wanted to know what was going on. After I told her, she told me to call the owners and get this straightened out. I gave the phone back to Jim's unfortunate wife and told her that she'd better call her boss. I knew what the owners would say to her. A little later, someone who worked there brought me a key to the pool gate.

I stopped by every morning and did a little bit of work at the retirement home. In my deal with the owners, they would sign that my one hundred hours were done when I finished the repairs. I really only worked about four or five hours. I now realize how community service works. You support a judge, and he gives you community service candidates.

A few weeks later I got a phone call from a friend. He said Jim Johnson, the husband of the woman who gave me trouble at the retirement home, was in Butch Krume's office. I had been looking for Jim because he owed me a bunch of money for some Oscars I had sold him. Jim had been avoiding me for some time, and I was pretty mad. I jumped into my truck and rushed over to their office. Jim saw me coming, and he ran out through the warehouse. It was a Friday, and a lot of their workers were waiting for their checks.

Running through the warehouse with me in hot pursuit, Jim made it out the back door.

As I chased him, a guy I went by and grabbed me and said something about me. I didn't know what he was talking about. I yanked myself loose from his hold. Then he hit me so hard I almost went down. I shook off the punch, and we had a fist fight. After exchanging a few punches, I knocked him down and pounced on him. With my left hand I grabbed him by the hair and put my right knee in his chest. I drew back with my right fist and started to knock him out, but thinking the fight was over, I didn't hit him again. I got up and started out after Jim. Before I got to the back door, someone else grabbed me from behind. I tried to break loose. Then he whispered in my ear, "I'm going to kill you." No one had ever said that to me before, and it sort of scared me. With all my strength, I moved a little to my left, and then, using my elbow, I hit him, and broke loose.

This time I was scared. We traded a few punches. I knocked him down again, and this time I did something I had never done before. As the guy tried to get up, I took aim and kicked at his head as hard as I could kick. I had work boots on. Thank God, I missed his head, but I had come so close, I might have killed him. It even scared everyone watching. A few of other workers grabbed me and said it was over. I never caught up with Jim, but a few months later I learned that while working on a pool, he was killed by a backhoe.

After finishing my community service, I was still being drug-tested, and Beverly, my parole officer, wanted me to build her a swimming pool. I still smoked pot and had to be drug-tested once a month or any time Beverly ordered one. When I went in for a drug test, I would have my son Danny, who didn't smoke weed, pee in a little plastic bottle. I would put the little bottle in my shorts, and then when I was supposed to urinate into a cup, Beverly would stand behind me and I would squirt the little bottle into the cup. She never caught on, and I never built her a pool.

In addition to the community service, the judge had also required me to attend a drug rehabilitation class which cost sixteen dollars a session. I went to class and decided to take it very seriously and get my money's worth. After the third session, the leader asked me to co-teach the class. That was fun.

Vegas

Demolition

In 1989, my friend, John Marshall, and his mother came to Vegas. The Flamingo Hotel was set up for demolition, and John had come to Vegas to complete a deal to get the entire contents of Bugsy Siegel's penthouse suite. To move the job along more quickly, John asked if he could use some of my employees. I had no problem with that so Matt, Tommy, Paul and I, all volunteered. John rented the largest U Haul truck in the fleet, and we all met one morning at the Flamingo hotel.

The penthouse had only two entries. One entry was from an elevator connecting the penthouse occupying most of the top floor of the three-story building to the parking lot in the basement.   The other was a narrow stairway leading from the basement to the penthouse.

Bugsy's penthouse was laid out with one large central room and several smaller side rooms. When we entered, the large room, we could see not only the whole room, but also we could look at any mirror and see everything going on inside the other rooms.

John had got us all official identification badges, and we began loading eight foot tall and four foot wide mirrors into the U-Haul truck. The mirrors, tied together with hinges, were heavy and awkward. John planned to build a room that would hold all the contents and furnishings from Seigal's suite, and that included the paintings, draperies, sinks, towels, bar chairs and seven stools. As we loaded the U Haul, we noticed a tall collection of box springs and mattresses stacked in the hotel lobby. Above the stack, a large chandelier consisting of intricate sparkling miniature lamps hung from the ceiling..

We were all wearing badges that made us look like we worked at the hotel. Waitresses, bellboys, dealers, and many others asked if they could climb up on the box springs stacked beneath the chandelier and get one of the little lamps from it.

"All right with us," we said. When we came back the next day we looked up at the chandelier, and it looked like a plucked turkey. We all laughed as we thought that whoever planned to get the chandelier was in for a disappointment. Matt still has the stools from

Bugsy's suite. Tom got some paintings and a television. I found out later that John had paid $8,000 for the contents of Bugsy's penthouse.

While we were making arrangements to get John's stuff, he entered his mother in a slot tournament. When we got back to the hotel, we went to find his mother who had just finished playing the slots. People were all around her. She had just hit the jackpot on seven slots in a row. She had won $15,000. That was in 1989. John and his mom came back the next year, and she won again, this time $11,000. The next year they came again, and she won again. This time she won $16,000. On the way home, she said, "Johnny, I think I missed my calling. I should have been a gambler." What do you say to a ninety-year-old woman who has won more than $30,000?

Pools and People

Over the forty-five years I lived in Vegas, I helped build a lot of pools. They included the rooftop pools at the Mint, the Rio, the Hilton, and Caesar's Palace.

At The Mint, we had to work at night. One night when the wind blew really hard, the hotel had scaffolding set up on the outside broke loose. Two-foot by twelve-foot long boards crashed down on Fremont Street. While trying to secure the scaffolding, my friend Bill Campbell's son fell to his death.

Next, we converted a scum gutter to skimmers in the Stardust pool, and we did the same to the Desert Inn's pool and the Sahara's pool. We tiled the Thunderbird, Tropicana, Sands, Hacienda, Bingo Palace, Showboat, Dunes, Circus Circus, Orleans, Treasure Island, Mirage, Luxor, Bally's and the MGM Grand. Now, some of those hotels and pools are gone.

The only job I did that I thought would last for years was the entrance to the MGM Grand. The entrance had a beautiful water feature dominated by the head of the MGM lion. The entrance to the hotel was through a mouth of the lion, but Asian people refused walk through the mouth of a lion. The hotel tore it out. That was a great disappointment to me. Over the years, so much of what I had hoped would last beyond my generation ended up being relatively short-lived.

The Dunes was demolished in November, 2007, then the Landmark Hotel and Casino was imploded in 2008. Steven Winn owned the Treasure Island. When the Dunes hotel was going to be imploded, Winn shot off the cannons at Treasure Island, and then set off fireworks at the same time as the Dunes was blown up. It was spectacular, as most of Steven Winn's ideas are.

Throughout my years in Vegas, I did work for Penn and Teller, Steven Winn, Liberace, Phyllis Diller, Roy

Rogers, Wayne Newton, Jerry Lewis, Sonny Liston, Sugar Ray Leonard and Mike Tyson. Liberace's pool waterline tile was like a piano keyboard, with white and raised black keys.

One of the biggest contracts I ever signed was the job for Siegfried and Roy. They had a fifty-acre forest just north of Vegas, and they lived in a two-story thatched roof bungalow with a small lake nearby. Roy's brother told me that Siegfried and Roy were having problems in their relationship. Siegfried wasn't coming around as much as Roy wanted, so Roy decided to give their place a facelift. Since I had been taking care of their other estate in town for about twenty years, I got the job of doing the water features. Roy loved his animals and had built big caves and all-tile pools for them to swim in and lounge in. It was truly a spectacular animal habitat. Now, Roy wanted to beautify his other animal kingdom. Roy, my son, Danny, and I got together, and Roy told us what he wanted. He wanted water clean and clear enough to raise trout and a solar-heating system that was efficient enough that his animals could swim. I told him I didn't have enough knowledge to handle this project. However, Roy told me he wanted us to handle what he wanted. I said we would explore his request.

Siegfried and Roy's animal sanctuary under construction

We asked around and found that the Riviera Hotel had a solar system for their water features. We found the hotel's engineer and spent some time with him. He was most helpful, and he taught us a lot about solar-power systems. When I had helped build Steven Winn's home pool and had gotten to know Elaine Winn, his wife. The Winns introduced me to an employee who took care of their water features. That employee also shared what he knew on the subject.

Eventually we went back and shared our new information with Roy who listened and then gave us the go-ahead with what he wanted. After the first few days we had a routine established. At nine every morning, I would meet with Roy and lay out the day's work. We had an employee named Tony, an extremely good looking young man who had a build like Charles Atlas, and that gave me an idea.

I took Tony aside and told him to wear his muscle shirt and cutoffs and to make sure every morning he was working in front of the porch where Roy and I would meet. Roy was gay, but not Tony. Even though I had worked for Roy for the past twenty years, he had never comped me in to their show at The Mirage. My strategy worked. Tony got comped three times while we were working on the project.

After about ten weeks we completed the job, filled the lake, and waited to see if we were successful. After about two weeks, we were disappointed. The water started to turn. Now, what would I tell Roy?

Roy didn't realize at this time we had failed, so I told my son, Danny, to get me a five-gallon pail of chlorine which we put in the lake in order to buy us more time to figure out what we could do. We investigated the water situation on their fifty acres, and it was very good news. The property was allotted a certain amount of water, and if they didn't use their allotment, they would lose it. Fortunately, there were three wells already on their property. We decided we could use the wells that were used to irrigate their property by pumping the well water into the lake. Then we would pump the water out of the lake for irrigation.

This would keep the water fresh and clear. It worked. We were all thankful, and Roy thought I was great. In spite of that success, I still never got comped to their show.

The Mafia

When I first moved to Vegas, I wasn't sure there was such a thing as the Mafia. However, it didn't take long for me to realize the reality of, "The Mob."

My first encounter with the Mafia was with a friend, Mike Fauci. Mike was in the pool business and needed a loan. I accompanied Mike to a little store near to Foxie's on the Strip. Mike went up to a little window, and they handed him an envelope with the money he had asked to borrow. Mike was Italian. As I found out, if you are an Italian, you have access to the Mob. Mike told me that if he didn't pay them back, he would probably end up under a rock in the desert.

My next experience with the Mob was personal. It started with a war between Tony Tagone at Tango Pools and Butch Krumme, a Vegas contractor.

Tango owed Butch money, and he refused to pay him back. In retaliation, Butch blew up Tony's dump truck. In return, Tony burned Butch's plaster rig. Of course, this battle made the news. At the same time, I was picketing Tango because – with Tony as owner – he also owed me money, about $85,000. I decided to get Tony's attention by following Tony every time he left his office. I wanted to scare the crap out of him.

One morning, as a reporter interviewed me. I told him that I thought, ". . .used car dealers were angels compared to most of the pool builders in Vegas." That was a mistake. That evening on the news, they used my quote. You can bet I received a lot of phone calls castigating me for what I said, and because of the publicity, the Mafia didn't like what was going on in the town.

Shortly after, I got a call ordering me to attend a meeting having to do with the money, Tango Pools, and me. We met at a restaurant on the strip.

When I got there, the table was filled with contractors that Tango owed money to, and Tony sat between two tough-looking men I had never before seen. They called the meeting to order and asked each of us subcontractors how much Tango owed us. We all gave the amounts he owed. The men took our receivables, gave them to Tony, and told him to pay us. They then looked around at us and said that the war was over. We all got our money,. Yes, we had the Mob in Vegas, and I'm glad they were on our side.

I had a friend named, Kenny. His wife's father, the head of a union, was killed by the Mob. My kids had a friend whose father was also blown up by the Mob. The last bombing I remember was the C.E.O. of the Stardust Hotel.

After that bombing, even though the C.E.O. of the Stardust Hotel lived, the Mob left Vegas. Now, big corporations own the major hotels. With the coming of the corporations, the price of hotel rooms went up and comps had all but disappeared.

Arizona Outings

Flagstaff Jail

Back in 2000, my brother-in-law, Pat Rogers, my dog, Dax, and I took a trip just north of Vegas to Viejo, Utah, to visit the lion hunter, Smoke Emit. Smoke and I had gone lion-hunting in the past and had become friends. During that hunt, I had bagged the largest mountain lion ever taken in the continental United States. My lion was even larger than the one Teddy Roosevelt took in 1901.

I never saw Smoke after that visit. He died of cancer caused by the fallout of the 1950's atom bomb tests set off above ground in the Nevada desert. The radioactive fallout caused cancers which eventually killed many sheep and people in Viejo, and Smoke Emit was one of the victims. The reason for this last trip to Viejo was to pay our respects at Smoke's funeral.

After leaving Viejo, Pat and I decided to make a side-trip to the Grand Canyon. Pat had never been there before. After we got on the road to the park, I got stopped for speeding. There happened to be a filming crew from the "60 Minutes," television program, and the police were patrolling the whole area.

When the police searched my truck, they found the guns we had with us. Then, when checking my driving record, they discovered a record of a speeding ticket I gotten ten years earlier in Nogales. I had thought traffic tickets were covered by the statute of limitations, but I was wrong. The police handcuffed me. Pat had not brought his billfold when we left so he had no identification. Since my pit bull, Dax, was with us, they let Pat go back to flagstaff on his own. I gave Pat my billfold and told him to meet me there. The police put me in their SUV, and we headed to jail in Flagstaff.

When we got there, I was stuck in a small, rock-walled cell that reminded me of something out of an old John Wayne western movie.

Eventually, Pat arrived with my billfold. I paid my fine, and they turned me loose.

In 1992, on another trip involving the Grand Canyon, my son Danny and I had to go to Meadview where I owned some land. After taking care of some business, we decided to go to the Grand Canyon. When we got there, we rented a helicopter and flew down to a Havasupai Indian Village at the bottom of the canyon and rented a room in the little hotel. After getting settled, we rented two horses and hired an old Indian guide.

We started our tour by going through the sad little village where we were staying.

We saw "No drinking" signs everywhere. Our guide told us that when the Indians started getting checks from the government, they gave up farming, and the little village almost dried up.

As the old guide lead us through the village, dogs barked, donkeys brayed, and kids waved at us. It was a beautiful little village with a large stream running down the middle where some Indians were fishing. We headed to the Havasupai waterfalls. We have all seen these waterfalls and ponds on calendars, but the reality was for more beautiful. We dismounted, and I looked back to see Danny lying on his back under his horse, perilously close to dangerous hoofs. When Danny had started to get off his horse, the ground had given way, and he had gone down.

On the trail to Havasupai Falls

We remounted and rode along on a narrow trail just above the falls. Danny wanted to climb down to the pools at the bottom of the falls, so we told our Indian guide he could go on back to his village because we knew the way back. After he left, we climbed down the walls to the pools below. We spent a few hours at the falls and then rode back to the village. We ate at the little village restaurant while we waited for our

helicopter ride out.

We spent a few hours at the falls

The Sweat Lodge

On another trip, to Kanab, Utah in 1993, my son Danny and I went to an Indian pow-wow. While there, we met an Indian who told us about a sweat lodge he was in charge of and invited us to experience it. We listened to him and decided to accept his invitation, and we went the next weekend. Afterward, we decided to go to the coral pink sand dunes which were not far from the sweat lodge. The next weekend we loaded our four-wheelers in the back of my pickup and headed back to Kanab.

Arriving at the sweat lodge about 4:00 in the afternoon, we discovered half a dozen others already there. We met with the Indian who had told us about this sweat lodge and learned that his Navajo name was Black Bear. As we introduced ourselves the Indians began moving hot rocks from the fire into the little lodge they had built. Soon we were told to undress down to our undershorts. I began to get cold feet. I gave Danny $100 and told him to give it to the Indian and then get out of there. My son looked at me in total surprise and said he wanted to stay and try it out. Reluctantly, I stayed with him. As the afternoon went on, I concluded this would not be my finest hour.

We were all herded inside the little six-sided lodge.   Inside, in the center of the floor, hot rocks sat atop a glowing fire. We had been given sagebrush branches to hold in front of our faces. When the flap on the door was closed, we sat in total darkness except for the red glow from the fire. Sitting on the sand floor, it became so hot I could hardly stand it. Black Bear began to chant, and we all began to sweat. I began to understand why people would hallucinate under such conditions. They poured water on hot rocks in the fire, and the steam made us sweat even more. Finally the flap over the entrance was lifted, and we literally rolled out of the lodge onto the cool pink sand. As I lay there, I discovered I was covered with sand fleas. Thank God they had a water house where we were able to wash ourselves off.

By now it was dark. We said our good-byes and left. With our two four-wheelers in the back of my pick-up, we headed for the coral pink sand dunes.

The road had a lot of dips in it, and I was in a hurry to get to our campground so I zipped along at a good clip. Topping a little rise, suddenly in the glare of our headlights, we saw eight cows lying down on the warm pavement. For an instant I thought we were dead. Seeing our lights, the cows started to get up. Desperately, I managed to zigzag around the cows without hitting any of them. Danny and I both knew it was a miracle we got through without hitting any of them. That night we camped at the coral pink campgrounds.

The next day I had one of the most exciting days of my life. I got to drive a three-wheeled ATV at a breakneck pace along a narrow trail. The terrifying part was that the trail skirted the face of a drop-off and then it went down the steep face. Trying to keep up with Danny, I was going way too fast for my limited skills and experience, but it was exhilarating, and I went on. We had fun that day.

Lake Mead

Early Saturday morning in 1993, the boys and I were off to Lake Mead to spend the day: three boys from my Sunday-School class, my son Matt, his uncle Pat and me. I had a new Sea-Ray inboard-outboard, and we intended to have some fun. We launched at the Lake Mead marina, and I planned to take the boys on a long trip to the upper basin. On previous trips, we always had often seen bighorn sheep. This morning was no exception. We approached and entered the long channel between the lower and the upper basin. I had navigated that channel many times, and I knew some neat little coves that we explored. However, when we got to the upper basin, and when we were about a hundred yards from shore, we broke down. I had a ski rope, and the larger boys jumped into the shallow water, took the rope and started pulling us to shore. We had water to drink but no food. I had planned to feed the boys at the lake restaurant, but since we broke down, our plans had changed.

We were stranded on the Arizona side of the lake about fifty miles from where I had parked my Bronco. I told the boys I would have to hitch-hike back to the marina. I didn't worry about leaving them because they could hike, swim and fish while I was gone.

I began walking down a gravel road, and it didn't take long until someone stopped to give me a ride back to the highway. Then I got another ride with some guys who were going to Lake Mead, and they took me right to the Bronco. I knew the boys would be hungry, so on the way back to pick them up I stopped to buy them some food at a Kentucky Fried Chicken restaurant.

On the way back, when I turned off the highway onto the gravel road, I noticed a large rattlesnake lying dead on the road. I knew it was a mean thing to do; but wanting to play a joke on the boys, I put the chicken in another box and placed the snake in the Kentucky Fried Chicken box.

When I reached the boys, I told them to start a fire because we needed to cook our dinner. When I opened the Kentucky chicken, they saw the snake instead of fried chicken. The littlest boy said he was really hungry, and he began to cry.

Immediately I told them I was only kidding and gave them the chicken. They soon forgave me.

Colorado River

In the forty-five years I lived in Vegas we often went to Lake Mead. When the lake was high we could easily go up the Colorado River. 1983 was such a year. My son, Matt and a friend, Paul, and I decided to go up the river as far as we could. As we worked our way up the river, every now and then we heard a strange sound, but with the other sounds of the river, the water swishing against the boat, and our own noises, we paid little attention to it and took in the beauty around us.

On both sides of the river, cliffs towered above us for more than a thousand feet straight up. We passed under the spot where the glass-bottom platform was later built, and tourists at the top of the cliff would be able to peer through the glass floor into the depths of the canyon below. Continuing up the river, we would hear the occasional strange high-pitched sound.

Moving deeper into the canyon, we passed a cable high up on the canyon wall. It stretched across the river from a large cave. The cave contained bat excrement, called guana, a valuable fertilizer. The cable had supported a cart used to extract the bat droppings from the cave. I remembered that George, my friend who had traveled with me to Israel, had worked in that bat cave for about six months in the 1950's. He told me they had built an elevator out of an old four-cylinder motor and some cable. They would sack the manure and send it down to the river and then load it onto barges that hauled it out. He said that while working in the canyon, they had planted and raised a garden and caught fish for their food.

As we continued traveling further up the canyon we kept hearing that high-pitched sound. Although we were running low on fuel, we decided to keep going. Since we were heading upstream, we figured we would use less gas going back, so we should be okay. As we approached the last large rapids, I was on my knees in the front of the boat so I could guide us around rocks and shallowest spots. Suddenly, Matt honked the horn. He said later that he had no idea why he honked the horn at that moment. However, he honked it, and I went flying forward off the bow of the boat. My belt caught a hook, and I was left dangling over the front. The water in the river was dark with silt. Some describe is as "too thick to drink and too thin to plow." For me, it was too thick to drink and too thin to chew, and I struggled back onto the deck.

Suddenly we learned the source of that elusive high-pitched sound.   Every time the prop of the boat grounded and chewed into the sandy bottom, it strained and whined. Now we had not only hit a sandbar, but we were high-centered on a big one, and we were stuck.

As we struggled to free our boat from the sandbar, a large river raft full of people came bobbing down the rapids out of the Grand Canyon. They helped us push our boat off the sandbar.

Deciding was no use to try to go any further up the river, we turned the boat around to start back, but we soon ran out of gas. Without power, we drifted along with the river current until we exited the river to come out on to the lake. We were about thirty miles from our vehicle, and we had no gasoline to get to it. Drifting slowly out onto the lake, we tried to figure out what we should do. Eventually, on the shore, we saw a camp and four or five trucks. There were also some four-wheeled ATV's and two beached boats. With a little paddle and a lot of sweat, we managed to beach our boat. We told the campers our story and then asked if they would sell us some gas. It was pretty obvious the campers thought we were pretty stupid to have run out of gas way out here. Then, refusing to take any money, they gave us what we needed. Grateful for their generosity, we all thanked them, and we were on our way home.

When we got home I found that my step-daughter, Cassie had been in a terrible accident at the lake.

I don't really know how this happened, but someone told me she was sitting on the stern of their boat and fell backwards into the water. She was caught by the propeller and held under. When she was helped out of the water, she had been terribly injured. The propeller had sliced from her vagina to her rectum. She was bleeding and had lost a lot of blood. They wrapped her in a beach towel and headed for the hospital. Thank God, she survived.

Unexpected

Encounters

Lead the Field

In 1969, Walter Arnold and I became dealers for the Nightingale Conant Corporation, a producer and marketer of a large variety of motivational material on cassette audio tapes.

We had flown to Chicago to a convention of the top salesmen in the U. S. to attend seminars featuring great speakers including Edgar R. Murrow, the great Second World War correspondent, and the memory expert Harry Lorane. At another seminar, we were with five hundred top salesmen. Before Harry Lorane was introduced to the group of salesmen, he went up and down aisle after aisle asking each of us our name. After he was introduced he did the most amazing thing I have ever been involved with. Even though no one in the audience of five-hundred salesmen had ever met him until then, he began naming each one of us. He went on to give a talk on "How to Improve Your Memory."

Clement Stone, a famous author and an advisor to President Nixon, was another speaker. In another seminar, we listened to a speaker who was a U. S. Senator.

Before this trip to Chicago, I had bought $45,000 worth of product. I guess because of that purchase I was elevated to one of the top salesmen. I told the top brass that I had only bought the product, but I have not yet sold it. I realize now they needed to make me a top sales person to help them inspire the troops.

As it turned out, I was lucky to be chosen one of the top salesmen because the top officials in the company paid special attention to us. They took us to the best restaurants, and what we were served were not simply meals; they were great feasts, reminding me of what the banquets of ancient Rome must have been like.

One evening about ten of us were invited to a dinner with Earl Nightingale in his penthouse overlooking the lake.

Earl was an American radio personality, writer, speaker, and author, dealing mostly on the subjects of human character development, motivation, excellence and meaningful existence. He was considered the "Dean of Personal Development."

Earl introduced us to his wife who had been an airline stewardess. As we ate, he shared how he gotten into this new business.

He had given a speech, "The Strangest Secret," to some top insurance salesmen. Someone in the audience recorded his speech on the recently invented cassette tape recorder. The guy made copies and started selling them for $50 each. That started the Nightingale Conant Motivational Corporation.

We both felt it had been a great convention, but we were looking forward to getting back home   As we drove to the airport the next morning, the snow was coming down hard. We got there on time for our flight and boarded our plane. However, we didn't take off.

At first our flight plan was to go to Houston, but their airport was closed. Then we were to go to Denver, but again, the airport was closed. Consequently we ended up sitting on the tarmac in Chicago for seventeen hours before they finally let us deplane and return to the terminal where we found all the restaurants and lunch-counters were out of food. At least we got to use a real restroom. All flights out of O'Hare had been cancelled.

After many hours, our flight was called, and we were on our way home.

Show Biz

Luke Harshman was a junior at Christian High when I was a senior. He was a friend of my brother-in-law, Clyde Kidd. Luke had changed his name to Bobby Hart and had become the lead in the group called The Monkees. Luke's girlfriend, Claudia Jennings, was a Playboy cover girl. In 1980 Luke and Claudia had come to Phoenix for my wife Chris's father's birthday.

During our visit, Bobby told us they had a cabin at Oak Creek, and he invited Clyde, Chris and me to join them. Delighted, we accepted. After a couple of days at Oak Creek, Bobby invited us to come to Los Angeles to visit for a few days. Again, we accepted the invitation.

In Los Angeles Bobby had a beautiful hillside home on a large lot with a swimming pool. He had just finished some work and his pool, and he wanted me to check it out because he was planning a pool party for the next day. I checked out his pool and found everything working properly. That evening he invited us over with some of his other friends. We didn't know most of them.

The next day as Clyde and I walked down to the pool, I was a bit embarrassed. The pool deck was full of naked women sunbathing. They were not at all embarrassed. I learned later that most of them were models for Playboy Magazine. There were no lighter areas on their bodies that bathing suits might have covered, and their tanned skins glistened from sunscreen. I guess it was typical "Hollywood." At that stage in my life, I didn't do drugs. However, there was plenty of pot and cocaine for the party.

One of Bobby's friends, Barry Richards, was the actor who played the monster in the movie, "Voyage to the Bottom of the Sea." Barry told us that he and Juliet Prowse were good friends and that if we ever went to see her show, we should tell the *maître de* that we knew Barry.

When we went to Juliet's show, and she sent a message back to us that we should meet her in her dressing room after she finished her show. When we came to her dressing room, we felt a bit awkward because all she wanted to talk about was Barry. After a little while she sent her love to Barry and we left.

Before we took our leave of Bobby, he called me aside and shared that he had fallen on hard times. He admitted he had spent too much money on foolishness. He went on to tell me that knew Burt Reynolds and had heard that Burt was making a new movie and needed investors. Deciding to take a chance, he had mortgaged his home and everything else he could beg or borrow to invest in "Smokey and the Bandit."

Fortunately for Bobby, the movie became a great success, and he made a lot of money.

I only saw Bobby only one more time. Unexpectedly, I ran into Bobby while on a trip to Rome, Italy. We were enjoying a meal in a nice restaurant in Rome when we saw Bobby with George Peppard seated at another table. George was escorting Bobby's ex-girlfriend. He introduced us, and we had a nice evening together. Bobby shared that his girlfriend, Claudia, whom we had met in Phoenix, had been killed in a head-on collision, and had been decapitated.

SUPER BOWLS

Raiders and Vikings

In 1977 I told my four boys, Danny, Matt, Travis and Bubba, that if the Oakland Raiders ever went to the Super Bowl, we would go. One of my best friends, Graham Reedy, was the doctor for the Raiders, and that year the Raiders were to play the Minnesota Vikings in the Super Bowl in Los Angeles.

Graham Reedy (left) and me at the Super Bowl

I drove over to Riverside, California to meet Graham at his sister-in-law Sarah's house. However, we had a problem. Graham only had two tickets for the game. At about 7:00 A.M. Sunday, the morning of the Super Bowl, Graham got a call from another Raiders doctor. Members of his party were still in Cleveland, Ohio and couldn't get out because of bad weather. We were in luck. Graham now had four more tickets. The game was to start at 12:30, but my four boys were still in Las Vegas. I tried the airlines, but they were sold out. I called the boys and told them the situation, and we decided they should drive. The Rose Bowl is in Pasadena, a little more than three hundred miles from Vegas. My son Danny had the best car, a Pontiac Firebird, so they decided to use his.

A little past eight in the morning, just four and one-half hours before kickoff, the boys left Vegas.

They paid little attention to speed-limits. With a CB radio in their car, and with the help of truck drivers, the were able to avoid the "Bears in the bushes," CB slang for cops on the highway. With his CB radio, Danny was able also to connect with other CB users who helped them find their way to the Rose Bowl.

I was a nervous wreck, but the boys made it in time for the kickoff. The Raiders won the game, and afterwards Graham took all of us down into the locker room for a great celebration.

Steelers and Rams

In 1980 the Pittsburg Steelers and the Los Angeles Rams played in the Super Bowl. My friend, Lee Looves, had two extra tickets, and he invited me and one of my boys to go with him. My stepson, Travis, was a Los Angeles Rams fan, so I invited him to go with us. Lee and his son Danny drove his car, and Travis and I drove mine. Again the Super Bowl was at the Rose Bowl.

We got to our seats just as they sang the National Anthem. When we sat down we noticed we were on the Steelers' side of the stadium. It was almost scary. Yellow towels were everywhere.

The Steelers were winning, and the fans were going wild. We saw a few fights in the stands. Travis and I were rooting for L.A., but we weren't yelling very loudly. In the end, it didn't matter. The Steelers won the game.   Even though Travis was a bit sad on the way home, we had a great time.

Chargers and Raiders

In 1981 I had season tickets to the San Diego Chargers game, and Matt and I decided to drive to San Diego and stay for the weekend with my sister, Imogene. On Sunday, we planned to go to the game where the Chargers were playing the Raiders. We left on Friday afternoon, and somewhere between Bakersfield and Barstow, California, I got stopped for speeding. The Highway Patrol officer gave me a ticket, and then we were on our way again. I watched in my rear-view mirror to watch the patrol car turn off. Then I rolled down my window and threw out the ticket. About ten minutes later I was pulled over again. It was the same Highway Patrol officers. They had me get out of my car and then handcuffed me. It seems I had a lot of unpaid traffic tickets in San Bernardino County.

Matt began to cry and wanted to know what was going to happen to him. The cops called for a tow truck and said they would take Matt too. As this went on one of the officers who was still sitting in his patrol car stepped out, walked over and started removing my handcuffs.

He told me I was a lucky man. After I got the first ticket at about ten till five, they discovered I had several warrants; but by the time they caught up with me the second time, it was after five o'clock. After five, they couldn't access my warrants, so they could not arrest me. As they unlocked my handcuffs, they told me again how lucky I was. This time when Matt and I left, I never drove over the speed limit, and we got to spend the night at my sister's house rather than in jail.

We spent Saturday with my sister, and on Sunday we went to the football game. Matt and I enjoyed the game; but we were losing, and Matt was almost in tears. At the last play of the game, wanting to cheer Matt up, I told him I would bet him ten dollars that the Raiders would win.

Because of this last play, the NFL later changed its rules. Dave Casper caught a short pass, and when he was hit, he fumbled the ball. After scrambling after it, he accidentally kicked the ball into the end zone and fell on it. It was ruled a touchdown, and the Raiders won the game. Matt was very happy to lose his bet.

Driving home from the game, I didn't get stopped for speeding.

I have been to California many times. I have never yet paid a ticket, and I had never yet gotten caught. But that came to an end.

For zipping through consecutive camera enforcement areas, I received three speeding tickets in December, 2016. I paid fines totaling $900 which included driving school fees. I decided my speeding days were over.

It took me a number of years to change bad habits, and abandoning speeding is among the least of them; for in looking back over my life, I was finally forced to face that what I professed to believe contradicted many of the behaviors and choices I made in my life. In the next section, I will explain the reasons for the change.

Part III

New Directions

I don't want to keep on a closet shelf

a lot of secrets about myself

and fool myself as I come and go

into thinking no one else will ever know

the kind of person I really am,

I don't want to dress up myself in sham.

I want to go out with my head erect

I want to deserve all men's respect;

From "*Myself*" by Edgar A. Guest

Sowing and Reaping

I had no idea that writing this book would cause me to take a long, hard, look at the way I have spent my life. Reaping what I have sowed has brought me both joy and pain.

Now, as Joannie and I read the Bible, pore over her Bible Study notes, or read together some edifying book, I truly rejoice that, at last, with Joannie by my side, we are endeavoring to serve our Lord.

For me, although my journey through life may seem awesome, it has left painful scars and jagged holes in my heart. As I worked my way through telling my story in this book, I was harshly reminded that there were extended periods in my life where I abandoned godliness, and in many ways became an outlaw, always defining "justice" in my own terms. Living life on my own terms left me with many regrets, and I am not proud of many of the things I did.

For years I struggled to find peace in my heart, and somehow, I always sensed God was there, but it was like I was sensing Him at a distance, through a sort of spiritual fog. With my many wrong choices and the actions that followed, I had alienated myself from God's guidance. Some have thought that I was more under the influence of the Devil more than under the Grace of God, and as I look back and catch "glimpses of my past" I can well understand their feelings.

In the sharing of my life's story – the good, the bad, and the ugly – God has opened my eyes to see myself far more honestly and clearly than I ever have before.

In spite of my poor choices and behaviors, God, in His mercy, has granted great good in my life. My children are drug-free, He has prospered me in business,

He has allowed me to have faithful friends, and He has given me the treasure of a wise and loving wife.

Twenty-five years ago, Joannie, my wife, became a Christian. Together, we have committed ourselves to serve Him wherever He leads and to do whatever He leads us to do.

The law of sowing and reaping, however, still applies. My heart breaks with the alienation between myself and my oldest son. That bond that once drew us so close together was torn, and I long for his forgiveness so that it might be repaired. I pray that someday, we will reconcile, and that my son and I will not have to mirror the last minute reconciliation between myself and my own father.

Some of the things I have written may well have offended some readers. I am sorry for that. It was sort of a frightening experience to reveal myself as I really am to myself, much less to others; but I wanted to leave an honest picture of the "real" Danny to my posterity. I hope they will understand, enjoy, and where necessary, forgive.

If we confess our sins, He is faithful and righteous to forgive us our sins and to cleanse us from all unrighteousness.

I John 1:9 NASB

Looking Back shows the real Danny Henderson from earliest childhood to his successful business in Las Vegas where for over forty years he built pools for the largest hotels on the Las Vegas Strip as well as for many celebrities. As his success grew, Danny always displayed a generous spirit and a remarkable decisiveness and energy; but along the way he encountered many personal, business and spiritual challenges.

In this painfully honest book, offering no excuses for poor decisions and bad behaviors, Danny lays all the cards on the table to tell the good, the bad, and the ugly. The reader sees not only Danny's love for people, but also his struggles as he worked his way through triumph and disaster.

The process of "Looking Back" in the writing of this book, Danny came to recognize the contradiction between his faith and his actions, and his life changed direction. He now goes forward as he concludes his story with, "I truly rejoice that, at last, with Joanie by my side, we are endeavoring to serve our Lord."

That God has worked that transformation in my life-long friend brings me great happiness.

— Pastor Pat Shaughnessy

$14.95

ISBN 978-0-9802279-3-2

51495>

9 780980 227932